Cricket All His Life

CRICKET ALL HIS LIFE

The Cricket Writings of
E. V. LUCAS

Introduction by John Arlott

THE PAVILION LIBRARY

First published in Great Britain in 1950

Copyright © The Estate of E. V. Lucas 1950
Introduction © John Arlott 1989

First published in the Pavilion Library in 1989 by
PAVILION BOOKS LIMITED
196 Shaftesbury Avenue, London WC2H 8JL
in association with Michael Joseph Limited
27 Wrights Lane, Kensington, London W8 5TZ

Series Editor: Steve Dobell

A CIP catalogue record for this book
is available from the British Library

ISBN 1-85145-188-9 Hbk
ISBN 1-85145-189-7 Pbk

Printed and bound in Great Britain by
Billing and Sons Limited, Worcester

INTRODUCTION

There can be a marked difference between a good cricket writer and a good writer who sometimes deals with cricket. Certainly the first may show deeper knowledge of his subject, but he will not necessarily please those with no great interest in it. The good writer, on the other hand, is a good writer – and that means a readable one – whatever his theme. E. V. Lucas was an extremely talented writer over a wide range of subjects but, though it represents only a fraction of his output, his cricket writing has charm and distinction and, simultaneously, carries conviction. He has two important cricket books to his credit. The first is *The Hambledon Men* (1907), the anthology he compiled and introduced on the theme of the Hambledon Club and its players. This was a most scholarly collection, remarkable for its polish as well as the intelligence of its research. It is beyond question an important contribution to the literature of the game. Then, not long before his death in 1938, he was asked to edit a booklet on the centenary of the Trent Bridge Cricket Ground, which he carried out as thoroughly, capably and felicitously as ever.

He had many literary gifts but it may well be that the deepest of them all was his capacity for enjoyment; an immense relish for many things. He shuffled them restlessly, as may be gathered from the fact that he attended eleven schools in the Brighton area before, at the age of sixteen, he became a bookseller's apprentice there.

Lucas was born to his Quaker parents in 1868 at Eltham in Kent, but the family moved to Sussex soon afterwards and he developed an immense feeling for that county which is reflected in many of his writings.

His religious upbringing was always reflected in his dislike of the seamy side of life, and his abiding belief that war was the greatest of all evils. He was, though, no puritan. Indeed, for many of his later years he was known as something of a gourmet; an enthusiast and a capable writer on the subjects of food and drink; and an extremely generous host.

At eighteen he left his bookshop and joined the staff of *The Sussex Daily News*. At twenty an uncle gave him £200 which he used to attend the lectures of that considerable scholar of English literature, W. P. Ker. An habitually voracious reader, he had already laid the foundations of his writing style. While still at his first newspaper, he diligently translated de Maupassant solely because he admired his style. (Which of those eleven schools, we may wonder, instilled that degree of literary perception?)

By 1893 he was working for *The Globe* and soon, also, for *Punch*, where he probably created his main reputation over many years of essays of outstanding quality. A portrait of him by Ralph Peacock hangs in the magazine's office. Lucas's standing was extremely high as a writer. He had a light touch and humour, innate good taste and a sharp eye for both character and literary quality. His ease of writing and touch concealed the immense skill of his work. He published more than thirty books of essays alone, recalling, to many, Charles Lamb who was, in fact, his idol. Some, indeed, have likened him to Lamb, but that does Lucas something less than justice for, while his writing had a somewhat similar charm, he had no such weakness of character. His seven-volume collection, *The Works of Charles and Mary Lamb*, and his *Life of Charles Lamb*, both published between 1903 and 1905, represent in some ways his most solid contribution to scholarship. He also, though, published monographs on painters – Vermeer and Constable – and travel books, not only on his loved Sussex but about Holland, Florence, Paris and France in general. He also toyed sensitively with the novel form, where his slightly acid sense of humour sometimes penetrated the romantic setting.

It is tempting to assess his effect on the writing of his

contemporaries and some who followed him. His work was widely available not only through *Punch* but in several daily and weekly papers, and his felicity, like that of Charles Lamb, must have found many echoes in the works of other writers. Certainly he was most highly respected in literary circles on several levels, an eminence recognised in 1932 when he was created a Companion of Honour.

The width of his interests – in people as well as subjects – and not least the pleasures of his table, meant that he had an unusually wide range of acquaintances, and many of them were friends. In the scope of his entertainment he was helped considerably by his wife, Florence – surprisingly, perhaps, the daughter of a United States army colonel (they had one child, a daughter).

This collection, made by that admirable publisher, editor and man of letters, Sir Rupert Hart-Davis, shows the width of Lucas's thought and interests even without going outside the realm of cricket – essays on history, terse, pointed anecdotes, jokes, poems, all indicate a man of many creative aspects. There is no typical E. V. Lucas: he was too many-sided for that, but a happy aspect of his perception, interest in cricket and general assessment of humanity occurs early here when he turns his attention to W. G. Grace: 'More than a figure, a landmark, for he grew vaster steadily, more massive, more monumental. What must it have been like to have that Atlas back and those shoulders in front of one in the theatre! At the big matches he would be seen on one of the lower seats of the pavilion with a friend on either side, watching and commenting. But the part of oracle sat very lightly upon him; he was ever a man of action rather than of words; shrewd and sagacious enough, but without rhetoric. That his mind worked with Ulysses-like acuteness every other captain had reason to know; his tactics were superb. But he donned and doffed them with his flannels. In ordinary life he was content to be an ordinary man.' Any professional writer would admire – even envy – a passage like that.

It is some measure of E. V. Lucas's distinction that now, virtually fifty years after his death, he is such an obvious candidate for an anthology; that so many people read, collect and respect him, and that his writing seems as fresh as ever. Rupert Hart-Davis confessed to having vastly enjoyed compiling this collection and that when he had completed it he found his admiration for Lucas even greater than it had been before.

It was Rupert who unearthed – though too late for the original printing – the item added here, entitled 'The Visionary Triumph' from *The Phantom Journal* (1919). It is a most happy addition, and gives this book, in that slight degree, the quality of a first edition.

In addition to his printed work, Lucas was a most felicitous letter-writer, who used frequently to write his letters almost entirely down the right-hand side of the page. He died a few days after his seventieth birthday, not long after he had completed some of the essays contained in this book. He had not only many literary admirers, he had very few enemies, and this book is a quite delightful memorial to both his literary gifts and his personal charm.

Alderney, 1988   John Arlott

CRICKET
ALL HIS LIFE

CRICKET WRITINGS IN PROSE AND VERSE

BY

E. V. LUCAS

Assembled and arranged by
Rupert Hart-Davis

'Last Munday youre Father was at Mr Payn's and plaid
at cricket, and came home pleased anuf, for he struck the
best ball in the game, and whishd he had not anny thing
else to do he would play at cricket all his life.'
                                        Mary Turner, 1789.

CONTENTS

CONTENTS

VIEWS IN VERSE

HOME AND AWAY

INTRODUCTORY NOTE

E. V. LUCAS was born in 1868, of Sussex Quaker stock. For most of his life he was engaged in the reading, writing, editing and publishing of books. He wrote on all manner of subjects, from Charles Lamb to the musical glasses: almost everything interested him, and in skimming through the formidable rows of his published works in search of cricket, I have once again been impressed as much by the wide sweep of his sympathies as by the grace and charm of his style. It is in the belief that cricket-lovers will welcome the gathering together of his writings on the game that, with the permission of his executors, I here present them.

His one and only cricket book, *Willow and Leather*, was published in 1898, but in 1907 he edited the famous anthology called *The Hambledon Men*. In this he reprinted Nyren's *Young Cricketer's Tutor*, together with other early records of the game, and linked them together with ample and lively comment of his own. I have found, however, that these pieces lose much of their force if they are divorced from their context, and I have contented myself with the account of John Nyren. The rest of my material has been assembled from the various books whose names and dates are given at the end of the extracts.

This volume does not pretend to include every word that E.V. wrote about cricket. A great many more must lurk in old periodicals, and even of the pieces which he from time to time reprinted in his books of essays and his anthologies, it has seemed politic to omit some altogether, and to abridge others, in order to avoid almost identical repetitions. The items here collected cover more than forty years of E.V.'s writing life, from *The Jubilee Book of Cricket* (1897) to *A Hundred Years of Trent Bridge* (1938), and it would be surprising if some of his favourite matches, scenes and phrases did not recur. As it is, the attentive reader will spot an occasional repetition which I have allowed to stand. For the rest, apart from the removal of a few score-sheets of early matches, I have done no violence to the texts, except to group them roughly according to subject and treatment, and to supply titles where these were lacking.

I believe that E.V. would approve of all this, and of the title I have chosen for the book. It is certainly true as a comment on his lifelong love of the game, and he himself placed the quotation from which it is taken on the title-page of *The Hambledon Men*. Moreover, when he later quoted this same phrase in the essay called *Winter Solace* (p. 113 below), he added the words: "There is the true spirit: 'All his life.' I too."

All his life he loved cricket, though he was perhaps more at ease in the pavilion than at the crease. True, he turned out on occasion for J. M. Barrie's team of writers and artists called the Allahakbarries, but when in after years his old skipper came to describe the side's triumphs in *The Greenwood Hat*, all he could find to say of our author's performance was: "E. V. Lucas had (unfortunately) a style."

As a spectator his style was all that could be desired. He watched cricket always with passionate attention, and if a large proportion of his writing on the game is concerned with "the backward look" and laments for past glories— and these are occupational failings in most cricket writers— let it not be imagined that E.V. neglected the living game of his own day. He was forever finding good reasons for slipping away to Lord's or the Oval, and on Test Match days his colleagues would have been as astonished to find him in the office as they would have been if the rest of the staff had turned up on a Bank Holiday. His affection for younger people often got them into trouble when he tempted them from their desks with invitations and Rover tickets.

He died in a London nursing home on the 26th June, 1938, while the issue of the second Test Match of that year, against the Australians at Lord's, was still undecided.

I owe a great debt of gratitude to E.V.'s old publishing firm, Messrs Methuen & Co Ltd, and in particular to Mr J. A. White, for his forbearance, generosity and assistance.   R. H-D.

GROUNDS AND PLAYERS

HAMBLEDON

HAMBLEDON lies in a trough among the Hampshire hills, in a valley within a valley, one side being Windmill Down and Broad Halfpenny Down the other. The modernising, sophisticating rail is above a league distant, and, save for weekly brake-loads of excursionists from Portsmouth, which is twelve miles to the south, the village sees few strangers year in year out. Approaching on foot from the east, you are upon Hambledon all unsuspectingly. Just when you had, perhaps, decided that the old place and its glorious traditions were, after all, but a figment of John Nyren's imagination, and that your pilgrimage was vain, there below you is the smoke of the Hambledon fires. The path downwards is steep and stony as one of Bunyan's toilsome ways, and a thought of Clovelly takes you here and there. At the foot is the George Inn, among other whitewashed houses, which stray as little as may be from the level road running along the bottom of the gulch. Looking around, and feeling a primitive peace in the air, you are persuaded it was worth the walk from Rowlands Castle to be at last in the nursery of cricket.

The George Inn, once the headquarters of the Hambledon cricketers—*vice* the Bat and Ball, deposed—but now possessing not even a relic of the game, is the chief hostel. Competition is, however, rife, for in Hambledon the inns are, after the good old English habit, numerically in all disproportion to the population, although, alas! no longer are their cellars deserving of the panegyric which once they won. These are bad days for the connoisseur of beer. No longer is such ale to be drunk as a hundred years ago moved Hambledon's historian to eulogy—"Barleycorn," he called it, "such as would put the souls of three butchers into one weaver; ale that would flare like turpentine— genuine Boniface! This immortal viand (for it was more than liquor) was vended at 2d per pint." Nyren wrote these words fifty years after the matches which were graced and ennobled by those libations were won, yet "the smell of that ale," he could add, "comes upon me as freshly as the new May flowers." The Hambledon men were ever good drinkers. The old Club book contains this illuminating entry: "A wet day. Only three members present. Nine bottles of wine." A wet day, truly.

Opposite the George a road starts up the western hill— Windmill Down—to the church. Here, under the long grass, lie some of the old Hambledon cricketers, whose deeds and characters live for ever in Nyren's pages. The path to the ground where once they played passes their graves. It is sad to think that these green mounds are nameless. A ruddy Hampshireman on the hillside above the church throws a light on the knowledge of the modern villager concerning Hambledon's tremendous history. Yes, he had heard say that the first cricket ever played was in Hambledon, but that was over there on Broad Halfpenny, a long while back. When he was younger they used to play every Sunday afternoon; they played for pints. Hambledon, by the way, never seems to have been quite willing to regard cricket as cricket's own reward. Stakes were pre- ferred. Sunday cricket is still an institution in the village, as it was in Kingsley's day at Eversley, and at Halton when Dr Parr dominated that spot. "Dr Parr," says Mr Pycroft, "on a Sunday evening used to sit on the Green at Halton (Warwick) with his pipe and his jug to see the parish lads at cricket, no one being allowed to play who had not been at church; the public-houses were deserted, and a better-behaved parish than the doctor's was rarely seen in those days." Such is the moral influence of cricket. Hambledon may not have reached this state of perfection, but cricketers and teetotallers alike will be pleased to know that the allurement of pints has ceased to be all-powerful.

Windmill Down is no longer meet for batsman and bowler. The slopes are yellow with corn, and the summit is divided between rank grass, growing from stony soil, with a profusion of high ox-eye daisies and purple thistles —such as Sir Horace Mann would have joyed to cut with his stick—and a copse of fir-trees and larches. But you can see what a ground for a hit it must have been in the old days, when David Harris, after infinite care, pitched his wickets on its turf. The view invigorates: but woe to the fieldsman who puts the pageantry of hill and cloud before the zest of cricket. A ball hit with any power—cut, as Beldham used to cut them, with "the speed of thought"— would, once it passed him, travel to the roots of the surrounding mountains. It was the making of fieldsmen. "The ground," says Nyren, "gradually declined every way from the centre, and the fieldsmen, therefore, were compelled to look about them, and for this reason they became so renowned in that department of the game." Nyren was once in with Noah Mann, on Windmill Down, when "by one stroke from a toss that he hit behind him we got 10 runs." Standing here, you can believe it, and if you have any imagination you can see the old farmers looking on, and hear again the deep mouths of the multitude "baying away in pure Hampshire—'Go hard! go hard! Tich and turn! tich and turn!'" The Hambledon Club's ground was changed from Broad Halfpenny to Windmill Down somewhere in the seventeen-eighties. The cricketers brought their turf with them and laid it afresh. Early in our century the ground was once more changed, this time to its present site, and once more was the turf removed. The turf of the present ground, which you reach by descending Windmill Down and then climbing a mere mound which lies to the north of it, is therefore (allowing for repairs) the same turf on which Beldham batted and Harris bowled a hundred years ago.

Harris and Beldham! Cricket records hold no greater names than these—Harris, king of bowlers, and Beldham, king of bats. On this very turf, so thickly sown, so springy, so fragrant (think of it!), David Harris bowled—Harris, who in All-England matches was the first man picked; Harris, a bowler "who between any one and himself," Nyren somewhat vaguely but enthusiastically says, "comparison must fail." David came from Odiham, in Hants. He was "a muscular, bony man, standing about 5 feet 9½ inches. His features were not regularly handsome, but a remarkably kind and gentle expression amply compensated the defect of mere linear beauty. The fair qualities of his heart shone through his honest face." This description is characteristic of Nyren. No man was more eager and glad than he to discover virtue in his friends and to celebrate it. Harris, "when preparing for his run previously to delivering the ball, would have made a beautiful study for the sculptor. Phidias would certainly have taken him for a model. First of all, he stood erect like a soldier at drill; then with a graceful curve of the arm he raised the ball to the forehead, and drawing back his right foot started off with his left. ... His mode of delivering the ball was very singular. He would bring it from under the arm by a twist, and nearly as high as his armpit, and with this action push it, as it were, from him." Lord

Frederick Beauclerk called David's bowling "one of the grandest sights in the universe." Like the Pantheon in Akenside's hymn, remarked the Rev. John Mitford, the friend of Lamb and a student of cricket, it was "simply and severely great."

Harris did not attain to his splendid heights without toil. "He was a potter by trade," said Beldham, "and in a kind of skittle-alley formed between hurdles he used to practise by bowling four different balls from one end, and then picking them up he would bowl them back again." And "you might have seen David," said another, "practising at dinner-time and after-hours all the winter through." "Many a Hampshire barn," declared the batsman Beagley, "has been heard to resound with bats and balls as well as thrashing." It is puzzling to us, who are familiar with Richardson's swinging arm, to understand how Harris acquired his speed in those underhand days, but all accounts agree that the potter's balls came in with terrible velocity. They rose almost perpendicularly from the pitch, and, said Nyren, "woe be to the man who did not get in to block them, for they had such a peculiar curl that they would grind his fingers against the bat." Mr Mitford, supplementing this passage, wrote with fine excess that the batsman's fingers would be "ground to dust, his bones pulverised, and his blood scattered over the field." And all the while David was beaming with his remarkably kind and gentle expression. Oh, a great man! Tom Walker, whom Nyren classes with the bloodless animals, although Beldham remembered seeing him rub his bleeding fingers in the dust, was alone undismayed. David used to say that he liked to "rind" him. None the less, Harris once bowled Tom Walker 170 balls for but one run, which proves Tom's imperturbability and powers of defence. "Gently,

B

potter, gently, pray," must have been (in the words of Fitzgerald's *Omar Khayyam*) the plea of the other batsmen. It was Tom Walker who "would never speak to any one, or give any answer, when he was in at the wicket. His tongue was tied, as his soul and body were surrendered to the struggle."

William Beldham, or "Silver Billy," as he was called, from his fair hair, was, with the bat, great as David Harris with the ball. He had "that genius for cricket, that wonderful eye, and that quickness of hand, which would," said Mr Ward and others, "have made him a great player in any age." For thirteen years he averaged 43 runs a match, and that at a time when 20 was a "long hand." A glance at *Bentley's Scores* will show you how consistent was this superb player. "One of the most beautiful sights that can be imagined, and which would have delighted an artist," said Nyren, "was to see him make himself up to hit a ball. It was the *beau idéal* of grace, animation and concentrated energy." "It was a study for Phidias," said Mr Mitford, "to see Beldham rise to strike; the grandeur of the attitude, the settled composure of the look, the piercing lightning of the eye, the rapid glance of the bat, were electrical. Men's hearts throbbed within them, their cheeks turned pale and red. Michael Angelo should have painted him." Beldham was the first man to run in to meet the ball. Others waited for it, and lost the chance of scoring, but he left his ground and scored. Mr Stoddart is his worthiest disciple to-day. "You do frighten me there, jumping out of your ground," said Squire Paulet, of Hambledon, remonstrating with Beldham. But Silver Billy knew best. Innovators must ever meet with opposition. Beldham did not invent the cut—that honour belongs to Harry Walker, brother of Tom—but he excelled at it. "His peculiar glory," said Mr

Mitford, "was the cut. Here he stood with no man beside him—the laurel was all his own; it seemed like the cut of a racket. His wrist seemed to turn on springs of the finest steel. He took the ball, as Burke did the House of Commons, between wind and water—not a moment too soon or late." When he could cut the balls "at the point of the bat," said Nyren, "he was in his glory; and upon my life their speed was as the speed of thought." No bowling came amiss to Silver Billy, fast or slow. Brown, of Brighton, who was a terrific underhand bowler in those days, bragged that he would bowl Beldham "off his legs." "I suppose," said Billy, "you will let me have this little bit of stick in my hand?" pointing to his bat. "He went in," says Mr Mitford, "and fetched above 70 against him." In after-years, when the old man was in his decline, Mr Mitford made a pilgrimage to Beldham's cottage, near Farnham, to see this little bit of stick. "In his kitchen," he wrote, "black with age . . . hangs the trophy of his victories, the delight of his youth, the exercise of his manhood, and the glory of his age—his BAT. Reader, believe me when I tell you, I trembled when I touched it—it seemed an act of profaneness, of violation. I pressed it to my lips, and returned it to its sanctuary." Mr Pycroft visited Beldham at Farnham in 1838, and afterwards incorporated much of the old man's conversation in *The Cricket-Field*.

The Jubilee Book of Cricket. 1897

THE INCOMPARABLE GAME

HAVING, the other day, once again spent an afternoon in watching a village cricket match, I am again perplexed by the passion for that game which is displayed by those who cannot shine at it. They cannot bat, they cannot bowl, they leave their place in the field, they miss catches, they fumble returns; and yet, every Saturday, there they are, often in perfect flannels, ready to fail once more. What is this lure, this attraction, that cricket exercises, and why is it that so few village elevens can ever muster more than two or three players who know anything? No wonder it is so hard for first-class teams to be brought together. As, the other day, I saw this lack of any kind of skilled resistance to the bowler, I meditated afresh on the difficulties of those observant pilgrims from green to green whose duty it is to build up the county's nursery; and as one defeated batsman after another, with a nought to his name and no sense of humiliation, sank into his deck-chair, I deplored anew the absence of national pride. Why on earth, I wondered, don't they watch better men and learn something? Why do they think they can hit before they have tried to defend? Why do they want to make four off the first ball? But so it is, and so it will be until September, when football again comes in, and if they make mistakes they will hear about it.

But the passion for cricket is in our blood. Small boys have it, youths have it, grown men have it, old men have it; and no amount of disappointment, no ducks, can change it. Even that scholarly cleric, the Rev. John Mitford, rector of Benhall, in Suffolk, collector, connoisseur and dilettante—he whom Lamb called "a pleasant

20

layman spoiled"—had it. In a man of letters so cultured you would not expect to see the spell of this unlettered game thus active; but it was there. Even as late in Mitford's life as 1827, when he was forty-six, we find Bernard Barton writing to Lamb a letter, now first published in a book, with these words in it:

"Mitford is gone crazy about cricket—he has, I am told, organized a cricket club in his Parish, and enters into its advancement and success with all the interest of an amateur. The Benhall Club (Benhall is Mitford's Parish) sent a challenge the other day to the Saxmundham Club—and the approaching contest was a matter of as much discussion in the vicinity as the Battle of Waterloo was some few years bygone among politicians. The Benhallites were beaten, and Mitford, so far as I hear, has [kept] house ever since. I fancy he has had a knock or two with the balls, for his letter talks of a disjointed thumb, a contusion on the hip, and a sightless eye; in another letter he describes himself as bandaged from head to foot, and as full of sores as Lazarus.

"In despite of all this he is a perfect enthusiast on the subject of bat and ball, wickets and bye slows. What is the Laurel, he asks, compared to the Willow? For that Tree alone makes good cricket bats; or the Myrtle to the Ashen? —of which the wicket, it seems, is fashioned. He apostrophizeth, anon, certain Cricket Players, just as he was wont to speak of Homer, Virgil, Dante, or Tasso. Poor M—I am sorry for his case: 'tis lucky we have a Lunatic Asylum erecting in the neighbourhood: but he may receive his quietus from bat or ball, and die ere his wits are wholly gone—and have this epitaph on his headstone:

> *Mitford! mighty once at cricket,*
> *Head erect, and heart elate,*
> *Now, alas! he heeds no wicket*
> *Save John Bunyan's wicket gate.*"

You could not have a better account of Mitford's fine
frenzy than that, and Lamb, although he liked Charles
Cowden Clarke and also Vincent Novello, who both knew
John Nyren, never refers to cricket and did not reply to it.
But Barton does not mention—what I happen to know—
the reason for this new excitement; and that is, that the
rector of Benhall had taken into his employ, but more as a
pensioner than a toiler, no other than William Fennex,
once an all-England player, and was fascinated by his
memories and enthusiasm. Indeed, had it not been for
these memories and enthusiasm the world would not have
had Mitford's articles in the *Gentleman's Magazine*, which
he edited, on Nyren's book, nor would Mitford's friend,
the Rev. James Pycroft, have written that other classic of
the game, *The Cricket-Field*, for upon Mitford's MS. notes
of Fennex's talk was it based. All honour then to the
"pleasant layman spoiled."

For a concise account of Fennex we have to go to
Lillywhite's *Scores and Biographies*, where Arthur Haygarth says that among underhand bowlers he possessed the
highest delivery ever seen, his hand, when propelling the
ball, being nearly on a level with his shoulder. I wish I
could have seen this. The few underhand bowlers that I
can recall kept their hands low, while Walter Humphreys
hid his behind a loose cuff. Fennex, in addition to being
especially good at single-wicket, and a very useful ally to any
side, was a pioneer in forward play. As we know from the
old man's own account to Mitford, it was when Fennex was
adopting this new but sensible method both of prevention
and cure, that Fennex's father, with the ordinary senile sus-
picion and dislike of innovation, cried out "Hey! hey! boy!
what is this? Do you call that play?" Fennex also has his
place in the history of cricket as the model for Fuller Pilch.

A blacksmith by trade, Fennex was 5 ft. 10 in. in height, muscular and abstemious, and even to the end he could walk prodigious distances. In conversation he was "facetious and comical." Leaving farriery, he kept a ground at Uxbridge, played for Middlesex, and had for a while the Portman Arms, Marylebone, where he used to smuggle tea. He was fortunate in his old age to be admitted as a titular gardener at Benhall and to have the custodianship of the ground at Eye. We have the Rector's evidence that it was Fennex's bowling, when he was between fifty and sixty, which removed the pride of Mitford and his young friends who thought they could bat. Elsewhere Mitford says that Fennex was still effective at sixty-five.

The Reverend John (who, I am told, was not over-burdened by a sense of fidelity to the Thirty-Nine Articles) was an enviable man in many ways. He had learning and leisure; his Suffolk garden was beautiful; his London rooms were comfortable; he wrote what he liked; but I covet nothing of his so much as the companionship, when-ever he wanted it, of Fennex, who was always ready to recall the past, and who in particular delighted in extolling the genius of Beldham. "He hit quick as lightning all round him," said Fennex. "He appeared to have no hit in par-ticular. You could never place a man against him; where the ball was pitched, there it was hit away." That was Silver Billy.

With a view to slimming, *Wisden* now omits from its preliminary list all cricketers who died before 1851, and Fennex, therefore, is not there; but you will find him in earlier issues as dying in 1838, aged about seventy-five, although Mitford says he lived to be eighty. There are, I find, some discrepancies in *Wisden's* revised list. John Nyren has, under the new rule, disappeared altogether, but Cowden Clarke retains an honoured place as Nyren's editor. I doubt if this is fair, for without Nyren there would have been no Cowden Clarke. Among other writers on the game whom I notice are Ashley-Cooper, Haygarth, Frederick Gale, Andrew Lang, John Mitford, James Pycroft, Stewart Caine, and three Pardons; but Denison, who wrote the excellent *Sketches of the Players*, is not there, and A. J. Gaston, who made some remarkable compilations, is not there.

Apropos the rector of Benhall, I have been looking at a number of the *Cricketer* which contains a reference to another enthusiast for the game who also was a Mitford—the late Francis William Mitford, aged eighty, of Wealden in Sussex, who dying, in 1935, after witnessing a peculiarly exciting match near his home, was found to have left a peculiarly interesting will.

After the usual disposition of his property, to descendants, relations, friends, servants and public characters, he adds:

"As one who has delighted all my life in cricket, at first as a player in my own small way, and later as a spectator, I wish to express my regret that the art of throwing the ball in from the field has so few adepts, both in the first-class game and in the club and village game. Even on county grounds it is habitual to see the wicket-keeper leaving the stumps, behind or beside which he should be rooted, and running several yards this way and that to receive the ball from slovenly fieldsmen; while in the smaller matches there is even less respect for precision. I cannot say when the art of swift and accurate throwing was allowed to decline; but I fear that it is no longer a matter for practice, and that when the young player has had his hour at the nets, either batting or bowling, he considers that he has done all that is needful. Even catching is not practised as it used to be and ought to be.

"It is in the hope that something may be done to bring back into English cricket such throwing as we see among the Australians, that I am directing my executors to set aside the sum of £500 to be divided into prizes to be awarded to the swiftest and most accurate returners of the ball to the wicket, from all parts of the ground, far and near, and in order that as many youths as possible may be affected by this incitement, I wish an announcement to be inserted in *The Times* at the beginning of the season following my death asking the headmasters of public schools and grammar schools who are willing to institute competitions to let my executors know.

"If I may offer any hints to the judges, I suggest that points should be given for direction, for speed and for trajectory, which should be low, the ball to reach the wicket-keeper's hands just above the bails either as a full pitch or long hop. A pound note might be the prize. It is not much, but no boy would despise it, and in the effort to win it a new spirit of keenness should arise which, in course of time, would reach the county grounds too."

A very ingenious scheme, which should bear fruit. I wish that a little of the money had been set aside for throwing-contests on the first-class field, but the testator knew what he was about when he chose the school for his arena. All the same, there may, here and there, be a generous patron of the game who, fired by Mr Mitford's example, will offer a fiver to be thrown for after an early end to a big match. The contests should be well worth watching and very stimulating.

Only the Other Day. 1936

TWO CRICKETERS

(i) ALFRED MYNN

ALFRED MYNN came of a race of Kentish giants, and was a giant himself. He weighed in his active prime nineteen stone, and towards the end twenty-four, and was over six feet in his stockings. The portraits of him are like those of a prize man at the Agricultural Hall. In one of them he stands flannelled and bare-headed on a village green, with a church—perhaps his own Goudhurst—behind him, a belt round his equator, a ridiculous little toothpick of a bat on his colossal shoulder, and a quiet smile (as of one who expected half-volleys later in the day, and would know what to do with them when they arrived) on his vast and kindly yeoman's face.

Nominally he was a hop merchant; but the great game was too much for him, and he allowed his hops to fend for themselves while he lifted their county to the highest place in cricket. (What are hops after all?) Like Atlas he carried Kent on his shoulders.

For twenty years he was the mainstay of the Gentlemen against the Players; and a great match in the thirties and forties without A. Mynn, Esq, in the scoresheet was less to be thought of than *Hamlet* without the Prince.

He bowled faster than any man in England, except, perhaps, Brown, of Brighton (who once bowled a ball right through a coat which long-stop was holding, and killed a dog on the other side), and he never tired. He "walked a few paces up to the wicket and delivered the ball like a flash of lightning, seemingly without effort". When he went in to bat he hit hard and he hit often, as great simple souls do.

He preferred fast bowling to slow, which is another sign of a lack of guile. In 1836 he made 283 runs in four consecutive innings, being twice not out. To-day we think little of this; but in 1836 it was almost miraculous, and I, for one, wish it was still.

Alfred Mynn's most famous single-wicket match was with J. Dearman, of Sheffield, on Pilch's ground, at Town Malling, for £100 a side. It was played on August 20, 1838. Frederick Gale was present, and he has left a description in his *Echoes from Old Cricket Fields*.

"A great portion of Mr Mynn's runs," he says, "were got by cover-point hits, though he lifted two balls apparently into some adjoining county. He scored in two innings 123 runs; and, if I mistake not, all Dearman's runs, eleven in number, were cover-point hits. There were only three wides in the four innings. Dearman was a little man, and Alfred Mynn looked a giant beside him. I can see him now in close-fitting jersey bound with red ribbon, a red belt round his waist, and a straw hat, with broad red ribbon. Dearman, who had never been beaten, and was heavily backed by the Yorkshiremen, had not the smallest chance with his opponent, and I verily believe that Alfred Mynn, out of sheer kindness of heart, gave him a few off balls in the second innings, as Dearman was 120 to the bad. The little man made some beautiful off-hits before the boundary stump, and was much cheered; but when it got near six o'clock, shouts of 'Time's short, Alfred; finish him off,' were heard from the throats of the lusty Kentish yeomen, and I have a vision in my mind of a middle stump flying up in the air, and spinning like a wheel, and perhaps if any one will go and look for it on the Town Malling ground, it will be found spinning still."

Alfred Mynn had countless friends and no enemies. How could he have enemies? He ate gigantic suppers, and

once kept Richard Daft awake all night with his snores.
When he died his noble body was escorted to the grave, at
Thurnham, in Kent, by the Leeds and Hillingbourne
Volunteer Corps, of which he was a member.

Let me add a sentence from Denison's *Sketches of the
Players* to complete the eulogy: "Gratitude for a kindness
displayed towards him is a leading feature in his character."

Good Company.   1909

[I cannot resist the temptation to round off E. V.'s words
on Alfred Mynn with W. J. Prowse's fine poem, particularly since E. V. himself adopted the same procedure
in *Good Company*. The poem was first published in *Bell's
Life* in 1861.   R.H-D.]

Jackson's pace is very fearful, Willsher's hand is very high;
William Caffyn has good judgment and an admirable eye;
Jemmy Grundy's cool and clever, almost always on the spot;
*Tinsley's slows are often telling, though they sometimes catch it
    hot.*
But however good their trundling, pitch or pace, or break or spin,
Still the monarch of all bowlers, to my mind, was Alfred Mynn.

Richard Daft is cool and cautious, with his safe and graceful play;
If George Griffith gets a loose one he will send it far away;
You may bowl your best at Hayward, and whatever style you try
Will be vanquished by the master's steady hand and careful eye.
But whatever fame and glory these and other bats may win,
Still the monarch of hard hitters, to my mind, was Alfred Mynn.

With his tall and stately presence, with his nobly moulded form,
His broad hand was ever open, his brave heart was ever warm;
All were proud of him, all loved him. As the changing seasons pass,
As our champion lies a-sleeping underneath yon Kentish grass,
Proudly, sadly, we will name him: to forget him were a sin;
Lightly lie the turf upon thee, kind and manly Alfred Mynn!

(ii) MR AISLABIE

"Mr Aislabie's wonderful good nature, pleasantry, and untiring zeal caused the eyes of all to be turned upon him in the cricket field." So says Aithur Haygarth, who had a very pretty reverence for this great man—great not only in sportsmanship and bonhomie, but great also physically, for towards the end of his life and his cricket career (which terminated almost at the same time: he was playing until he was sixty-seven and he died when sixty-eight, in 1842) Mr Aislabie weighed twenty stone, and had a man not only to run for him when batting, but to field for him too—just as David Harris was provided with an arm-chair into which to subside after delivering the ball. But even although Mr Aislabie's part in the game was so vicarious and his stay at the wicket so short, to have left him out of a match in which he was willing to play would have been wantonly to eclipse the sun. For where Aislabie was were high spirits and good fellowship of the best.

He was born in 1774 in London and educated at Sevenoaks and Eton. He then became a wine merchant and West India merchant, and took Lee Place in Kent, its owner and which together were known facetiously among his friends as "The Elephant and Castle." Cricket was his passion, although he was never much good in any department of the game. Nevertheless, as I have said, he played all his life, often in first-class matches.

Though later Lord's was his official cricket home, for he was honorary secretary of the M.C.C. for twenty years, Mr Aislabie's happiest and least responsible days in the field were with the West Kent cricketers, of whom Mr Philip Norman some few years ago wrote such a delightful history. That comely and substantial volume might in-

deed be called the epic of Aislabie, since Aislabie's vast
jocose form dominates it, while its pages are continually
bubbling with his convivial rhymes. For Mr Aislabie was
not cricketer alone; he was the Club's authorised Bacchus
and the Club's self-constituted Laureate. After every
match the eleven first drank Aislabie's port (a pint to every
man), and then listened to their vintner's irreverent verses
on the day's play. He missed nothing. Mr Aislabie employed that very useful medium for the satirist, the
rhymed alphabet, which he managed very cleverly, getting
a boundary into every line. The Z—that stumbling-block
to most alphabeticians, who usually decline weakly on
"Zany"—he managed too, like a man and a wine merchant.
Thus:

> *Y was Yoicks Lockwood, hark to him, Blue Mottle!*
> *Z—that Z bothers me; push round the bottle!*

Like a sensible cricketer and convivial poet Mr Aislabie
did not force his Pegasus to take difficult hedges; he allowed
liberty of action, and the rhymes are often faulty and the
metre faulty too. But the spirit! Here is a stanza from a
song on a match between the Gentlemen of Kent and the
M.C.C. in 1833:

Charley Harenc loves good wine, Charley loves good brandy,
Charley loves a pretty girl, as sweet as sugar-candy.
Charley is as sugar sweet, which quickly melts away, sir,
Charley therefore stops away on a rainy day, sir.
Charley knocks the knuckles of many an awkward clown, sir,
If Charley stops away again, he'll chance to rap his own, sir.

Here the poet was getting home a little, for it seems that
Harenc had been down to play at Lord's recently, but
because it rained at Chislehurst he was some hours late,
whereas it did not rain at Lord's at all. Like a true satirist
Mr Aislabie was always smilingly rubbing in the salt. For

example, after R. W. Keate in three successive innings had been bowled for nothing by Alfred Mynn, and had been defeated at single wicket by J. L. Langdon, he wrote the following quatrain, in which "b Mynn o" must be pronounced as a dactyl:

> B Mynn o—b Mynn o—b Mynn o Keate
> Tried with his bat jolly Langdon to beat.
> In vain, for with Langdon can never compete
> B Mynn o—b Mynn o—b Mynn o Keate.

Here is one of Mr Aislabie's stanzas, wholly in praise, upon the father of the late Mr Jenner-Fust:

> There is a man at Chislehurst, of whose whole life the tenor
> Is kindness and benevolence. Who's that? Sir Herbert Jenner.
> He such a hearty welcome gives, and such a splendid dinner,
> That even if I lose the match, I still shall be the winner.

At Eton Aislabie was adored, and for many years it was the custom to give the captain of the eleven the great man's portrait, with the names of the team written on the back. It may be so to-day, but I imagine not. He figures also historically at another school, for Hughes described him in *Tom Brown's Schooldays* as the organiser of the M.C.C. team against Rugby: "in a white hat, leaning on a bat in benevolent enjoyment"—a fine phrase. To have a crack with Aislabie took, one fancies, as many people to the pavilion at Lord's almost as to see the match. That building holds a permanent souvenir of him in the shape of a bust. The first stone of the old tennis court there was laid by his hands.

Mr Aislabie died in 1842, and was buried in the parish church of Marylebone, but the tombstone above his wife in Sevenoaks churchyard bears his name. He might justly be called the Father of club or house-party cricket.

Good Company. 1909

TWO CRICKET GROUNDS

(i) THE OVAL

To thousands of Londoners who live north of the river there is only one transpontine resort, and that is the Oval. I am of this number. How rarely we cross the river, except in trains on our way to the coast or to the southern counties, it is absurd to think. But to the Oval, in one of the great London County Council dreadnought trams, which start from the Embankment, or in the friendly taxi after lunch, or by that convenient Tube which disgorges its eager passengers only a few yards from the chief gates, how often do we hasten!

The difference between an Oval crowd and a Lord's crowd is immense. Being nearer the fashionable areas, and having the Eton and Harrow match and the Oxford and Cambridge match, those favoured opportunities for the modiste, Lord's has not only a cricket public but a butterfly public. And this means not only awnings and comfort but a more careful standard of male attire too. The Oval crowd is far liker a football crowd. It is almost wholly composed of men, and men who must earn their living, and their keenness is not only far more articulate than any at Lord's, but greater too. Indeed it must be so, or they would not stand for hours, as they can in August, on the surrounding cement banks, with no shade whatever, or welcome in the new season on an Easter Monday, as I have seen them, in a breeze direct from the North Pole; and how some of them can see at all is a mystery, for the Oval is far larger than Lord's, there being a possibility (I have often seen it realized) of making 5, all run, in at least two parts of the ground. But the Oval crowd is not to be dissuaded by weather or discomfort, and the packed roof of the neighbouring inn, between the overpowering gasometers and the Pavilion, gives the scene just that old-fashioned touch that is so agreeable. Something of the kind one has noticed in old prints of prize fights in the days of Cribb, or of Newmarket Heath before all the modern mechanical devices came in and S.P. were still meaningless initials.

The pavilion is different too; which is only natural, for the pavilion at Lord's is the Houses of Parliament of cricket, whereas the pavilion at the Oval is merely the pavilion of a county ground. But hardly less interesting are its pictures and records; one of the pictures is a fascinating early match painted by George Morland.

One reason which endears the Oval to me is that the season dies harder there than elsewhere. That last big match of the year, when the September hazes have begun, between the champion county and the rest of England, is always played on the Surrey ground, and I always try to be present. I have too the pleasantest recollections of Gentlemen v. Players matches at the Oval, because Lord Harris always sends a huge basket of Kentish Whitehearts to cheer this event, and these, through a fortunate acquaintance with two or three famous hands who have of late been participators, I have had the felicity of tasting. There are notoriously no cherries like them.

Kennington Oval existed long before it was a cricket ground, and Surrey existed as a cricket county long before that. Surrey indeed took to cricket as early as any county, except, I suppose, Hampshire, where the Hambledon Club was. One of the first matches recorded in Lillywhite's *Scores and Biographies* (the best of all books) is between

c

Surrey and Kent on the Laleham-Burway ground at
Chertsey in 1773. The match was so memorable that the
Vicar of Sundridge, the Rev. J. Duncombe, celebrated
it in a ballad in the manner of *Chevy Chase*. No other
literature of the game gives a better idea of the fun and
want of scientific precision about it in those early days. To
a large extent the interest seems to have centred in wagers
on the result, between the Earl of Tankerville, who played
for Surrey, and Sir Horace Mann, who played for Kent.
Surrey won. Says the reverend poet:

> *Of near three hundred notches made*
> *By Surrey, eight were byes;*
> *The rest were balls which, boldly struck,*
> *Re-echoed to the skies.*

At the end of his poem the Vicar reverted to type and
worked in a moral:

> *God save the King, and bless the land*
> *With plenty and increase;*
> *And grant henceforth that idle games*
> *In harvest-time may cease.*

Surrey seems to have been beaten in the return match,
this time at Sevenoaks; but Lillywhite does not give it.
Later in the year they met yet again, at Canterbury, and
Surrey again won. On the first and third occasions, at any
rate, Surrey had the famous Lumpy to help them; and a
poem composed on the third conflict said roundly that

> *Surrey did the victory gain*
> *By Lumpy, fortune, art and rain.*

After this the next mention of Surrey by Lillywhite is on
July 20, 1774, when, with the assistance of the borrowed
Minshull, they played the Hambledon Club and lost—

this borrowing of one or two men, to equalize the sides, being very common in those days. In the next recorded match, Surrey, against the Hambledon Club, again at Chertsey, on July 6, 7 and 8, 1775, had the services of Miller as well as Minshull. Surrey won. On July 13 a return began, at Hambledon, which Hambledon won by 296 runs. J. Small was the hero: for in the second innings he carried his bat for 136. So much for the beginnings of Surrey cricket.

The present ground dates from 1845, when, in March, the first turf of the ground that we now know was laid. Before that it had been for long an open space, partly field and partly market garden.

The Montpelier Club, the principal South London Cricket Club, which had played its matches on the Bee-Hive Ground, in Walworth, being turned out by the builders, decided in 1844 to move to the Oval. Early in 1845 a meeting was called to consider the future, over which Mr William Ward, whom we meet in the Lord's chapter, presided. Among those present was the great Felix. Another of the company was William Denison, who wrote an informing book entitled *Sketches of the Players*. At this meeting it was decided that the Montpelier Club should disappear and a Surrey Club be formed. Later in the year a second meeting was held at the Horns Tavern, which is still a famous house, preceded by a dinner. On this occasion the late Lord Bessborough, who is known in cricket annals as the Hon. Frederick Ponsonby, took the chair; and the merging of the Montpelier Club into the Surrey Club was practically settled, seventy members of the old club enrolling themselves in the new.

For a while the Surrey Club did not prosper, owing to various difficulties with the lessees of the ground, but in

1857 a smoother course was secured and thenceforward all went well. The first real pavilion was built in 1858, and in that year Surrey, with Sussex to help, beat England twice. Of more recent history it is unnecessary to speak.

A word or two of William Denison, the first secretary of the Surrey Club, whose *Sketches of the Players* appeared in 1846. A cricket enthusiast of the deepest dye, he was described by Lord Bessborough, in a letter to Bishop Montgomery, whose *History of Kennington* has some most attractive chapters on cricket and Surrey cricket, as "the best bowler in the Montpelier Club, the first man who had the pluck to bowl round-arm slows in good matches". Denison was otherwise a *Times* reporter on law and parliament, and a cricket journalist, and so busy a man could hardly do justice to the requirements of a new club in not too prosperous circumstances. From the dedication of his book to the Noblemen and Gentlemen of the M.C.C. one gathers that he had his feuds. He writes:

"It has, I hear, been asked how it comes to pass that I should have *presumed* to *arrogate* to myself, as the parties have termed it, the privilege of suggesting alterations in the rules by which the game is regulated, thus assuming a knowledge of their working superior to the majority of those who have for many years taken an active part in its practice; and therefore I shall, I trust, be pardoned, if I state the position I have held in cricket since 1813. In that year it was solicited that I (at the period a lad) should be permitted, in the absence of a good player, to play in a match at Richmond between the 'Counties of Middlesex and Surrey'. The permission of the Reverend Gentleman under whose tutelage I then was, having been accorded, I made my appearance, then, as now, a *slow bowler*, in the 'Surrey Eleven'. From that day to the present I have devoted the largest portion of my unoccupied time to cricket, and from the year 1816 there has been no season in which I have not witnessed nearly every match of importance, nor in which I have not been a *playing* member of *four* and frequently of *nine* clubs, and even at the present moment I remain an active participator in *five*. The consequence then was that being attached to the game, and compelled, by the state of my health, to resort to strong out-of-door exercise, I have probably witnessed, played in, and contributed to, in a pecuniary sense, a greater number of matches than anyone who is now to be found in the cricket ranks. The result has been, that there is no class of match, high or low, in which I have not constantly been engaged. Moreover, it has been a portion of my public duty to contribute articles on cricket, and to attend and write notices of matches for the Press, since 1820."

As an afterthought to the dedication comes this amusing P.S.:

"In answer to a remark which I overheard at Lord's last summer, 'that Mr Denison could not know much about the game, because he obtained so few runs', I beg to suggest that the dislocation of an elbow, met with at cricket, and an impaired vision, arising not merely from surgical operations, for I have had eleven on one eye, but an average of bed of not quite *four* hours per night, for twenty-six years, are somewhat calculated to spoil a man's sight for hitting. Some years back, and for many years, there were few gentlemen whose batting or bowling average stood better."

To the Oval, belonging as it does to the Duchy of Cornwall, and therefore to the Prince of Wales, such servants of the Crown as soldiers, sailors and postmen are admitted free. In 1851 a very serious attempt was made to get the ground for building purposes, but it was resisted mainly through the action of the Prince Consort, who was administering the estate for his son. This fact should be emblazoned on the Albert Memorial.

I have mentioned the raised cement banks that surround the Oval and give a view to all. They were made by the contractors who undertook the draining, or rather hiding within pipes, of the river Effra, which, until 1880, ran by the side of the Oval into the Thames at Lambeth. When it was removed from sight the excavated earth was piled all round the ground and cemented over. The Chelsea football ground, whither the King and a vast number of his loyal subjects, including myself, journeyed a few winters ago to see an American baseball match, obtained its high banks in a similar way, for they are made of the earth excavated for the London Tube railways.

One little piece of special Oval lore I can impart. Near Vauxhall Bridge Station there is a church, and this church has an open space, or unglazed window, in its spire. If the light through this window, as seen from the Pavilion, is clear, there will be no rain; but if one can only just see through it, rain is likely.

Every one has his favourite county ground memories. Among the later ones of mine, at the Oval, is that innings of deadly resistance and care by Mr Fry which saved England from Australia in the test match rubber of 19—. Another is a hit by Mr V. F. S. Crawford on to the roof of the pavilion. And I can see again Richardson sending down one of his terrific bailers, and Hobbs's effortless boundaries, where the bat became a shining blade, and Hayward's gentle strokes for one as he grew older and found running less to his taste. But the most inspired cricketer of the Oval in our time was George Lohmann.

(ii) LORD'S

The first match played on the present Lord's ground, according to Lillywhite's *Scores and Biographies*, was on

June 22, 1814. The sides were the M.C.C. v. Hertfordshire (with Mr Bentley). The M.C.C., for whom those early giants, Lord Frederick Beauclerk, Mr Budd, Mr (or "Squire") Osbaldeston, and Mr William Ward, were playing, won. The second recorded match on the present ground was of a kind now unhappily extinct: single wicket. It was on July 4, 1814, and the sides were the four Hampshire men, E. Carter, Thumwood, John Bennett, and T. C. Howard, against the three M.C.C. amateurs I have named above, with the Hon. E. Blyth (of Kent) added. The gentlemen won handsomely—and so the ground's glorious career began.

Its history is this. In the latter half of the eighteenth century, when cricket began to make its way, London had but one cricket club of any standing, the White Conduit Club, called sometimes the Star and Garter, which numbered among its members many jovial spirits who were as ready for a practical joke as for the game, but none the less helped to revise the laws of cricket in 1755 and 1774. Among the members was the eighth Earl of Winchilsea, a very keen hand, who retained in his service a capable all-round Yorkshireman, named Thomas Lord, to be useful in many ways, and not the least in bowling to gentlemen. One day in the seventeen-eighties the Earl of Winchilsea suggested to Lord that there would be plenty of support forthcoming if he would make a ground in a more central position than the White Conduit, and keep it more select, so that the genial amateurs of cricket might be sure of being able to get a knock (as we say now, and as was practically all that batting meant then) whenever they liked.

Lord expressed himself as willing, provided he could be guaranteed against loss; and the Earl and his friend Charles Lennox, afterwards fourth Duke of Richmond, promising to see him through, set to work, and the ground was ready in May, 1787, the club which was formed to play there and support it being called, after the parish in which the ground was situated, the Marylebone Cricket Club. Such was the light-hearted inception of what has grown to be the vast and highly organized institution which all men know and respect as the M.C.C.

Lord's first ground occupied a site of which Dorset Square is at present a part. That was from 1787 until 1810. Having notice to quit, he acquired a new ground at the top of Lisson Grove, where the Great Central Railway now is; but, the Regent's Canal being planned to run right through it, he had again to move, and this time he settled in St John's Wood and remained there. The story which always used to be told was that Lord each time carried his turf with him; but that cannot be true if, as the centenary history states, the second ground was being played on for two years—1808–1810—before the first was given up. It was, as I have said, in 1814 that the present Lord's ground was ready.

Thomas Lord remained in control of the ground until 1825, when, his lease being up, that enemy which is always threatening the prosperity of any open space in a big city began to draw nearer—I mean, of course, the builder—and very drastic steps were necessary. To his assistance came Mr William Ward, perhaps the greatest benefactor that cricket ever had, and one to whom, were London's statue-raising zeal thorough, there would long since have been a monument, for he practically, as we have already seen, was the father of the Oval, too. This most fortunate blend of the sportsman, the financier and the patriot, was born in 1787 and educated at Winchester. He grew to be six feet one inch, weighed fourteen stone, and played with a 4-lb. bat. In 1820 he made 278 in an innings; which long remained the second highest score. He bowled slow under-hand, kept himself on too long, and fielded at point. He played cricket almost to the end of his life, chiefly for the M.C.C. and Hampshire, and was one of those to take a reasonable view when round-arm came in. Mr Ward being also a Director of the Bank of England and M.P. for the City of London, it was natural when Lord saw difficulties threaten that he should turn to him.

The result was that Mr Ward bought the lease, which in 1835 he transferred to James Henry Dark of honourable memory, who held it until 1864, when the Club became the owners of the ground. Dark, however, continued his active participation in management for several years and is hardly less the hero of its history than Thomas Lord himself.

Not the least valuable portion of the volume—indeed, it might well be considered the most valuable since it em-bodies the personal recollections of a great cricket en-thusiast and patron, whose unclouded memory could go back for four-score years—is the late Sir Spencer Pon-sonby-Fane's introduction. Sir Spencer, who died in 1915, is another example of the happy longevity that can be the lot of followers of the greatest of games; for he lived to be ninety and thus comes within easy distance of his old friend Mr Jenner-Fust, who lived to be ninety-nine, and William Beldham, who was ninety-six; while his friend Mr Budd reached ninety. Sir Spencer first knew Lord's in the eighteen-thirties at the beginning of the Dark régime. He thus describes it:

"In the then Pavilion, a small one-roomed building, surrounded with a few laurels and shrubs, and capable of holding forty or fifty members, I can see Mr Aislabie, the Secretary of the Club, a big fat man over twenty stone in

weight, fussing about with a red book in which he was
entering subscriptions for some desired match of which the
funds of the Club could not afford the expense. And here
sat Lord Frederick Beauclerk, then the Autocrat of the
Club, and of Cricket in general, laying down the law and
organising the games. On these he always had a bet of a
sovereign, and he himself managed them while sitting
alongside the scorers at the top of the ground, whence he
issued his orders to the players. He himself had then given
up playing.

"Round the ground there were more of these small
benches without backs, and a pot-boy walked round with a
supply of Beer and Porter for the public, who had no other
means of refreshing themselves. Excepting these benches
there were no seats for spectators. At the south-west
corner of the ground there were large stacks of willow-
blocks to be seasoned and made into bats in the workshop
adjoining. On the upper north-east corner was a large
sheep-pen. In the centre of the ground, opposite the
Pavilion, was a square patch of grass which was kept constantly rolled and taken care of. No scythe was allowed to
touch it, and mowing machines were not then invented.
The rest of the ground was ridge and furrow—not very
easy for fielding on, nor made any easier by the number of
old pitches which abounded, for on non-match days the
public could have a pitch for a shilling, a sum which
included the use of stumps, bat and ball, the last-named
selected from half a dozen or so from the capacious breeches
pockets of 'Steevie' Slatter, Mr Dark's factotum, which
never seemed to be empty.

"The grass, as I have said, was never mowed. It was
usually kept down by a flock of sheep, which was penned
up on match days, and on Saturdays four or five hundred
sheep were driven on to the ground on their way to the
Monday Smithfield Market. It was marvellous to see how
they cleared the herbage. From the pitch itself, selected by
Mr Dark, half a dozen boys picked out the rough stalks of
the grass. The wickets were sometimes difficult—in a dry

north-east wind, for instance; but when they were in good order it was a joy to play on them, they were so full of life and spirit. The creases were cut with a knife, and, though more destructive to the ground, were more accurate than those marked subsequently with white paint!"

"Let us now praise famous men", is the real motto of any cricket history. And what a procession of heroes Lord's can remember! The Earl of Winchilsea, the father of the M.C.C.; the Earl of Tankerville, who employed Nyren's Lumpy (and, as we have seen, Surrey's borrowed bulwark) as his gardener and Bedster as his butler; the Duke of Dorset, who kept Miller, Minshull, and Bowra, all worthies of Nyren's deathless page, in his service, handy for the game; Sir Horace Mann, who retained the brothers Ring; The Rev. Lord Frederick Beauclerk, D.D., who seems, in spite of his passion for cricket and fine aptitude at it, to have done as a "backer" his best or worst in the impossible task of ruining its character; Mr Budd, "who always wanted to win the game off a single ball", and "did so like to make the ring fall back farther and farther as he warmed to his play"; Mr Ward himself, who used the same bat for fifty years, and as he grew older is said, while standing nominally at point, to have treated the striker with too much respect—and who can blame him? George Anderson, who, when he could not sleep, went downstairs for his bat and took it back to bed with him; Mr Benjamin Aislabie, who composed comic rhymes on his contemporaries and was never refused a subscription to a match; "Squire" Osbaldeston, who bowled so fast that he required two long-stops; Will Caldecourt, who hit six 6's in an over; Mr Kingscote, who drove Lillywhite out of the ground into Hanover Crescent; William Lillywhite himself, who to his Captain's reproaches for not catching someone off his own bowling—the "Nonpareil" being very chary of injuring his hand—replied definitely, "Look here, sir, when I've bowled the ball I've done with her, and I leaves her to my field" (pronouncing bowled to rhyme with fouled); Mr C. G. Taylor, a wag as well as a cricketer, who backed himself to learn the piano and sing, in six weeks, and walk down King's Parade in a pair of trousers of his own make, and won; Old Clarke, the slow bowler, who forewarned the field of any impending "haccident"; the great Alfred Mynn, the Kentish colossus, perhaps the finest figure in the whole history of the game, who, when there was a question of increasing the number of balls in the over said, "Myself, I should like a hundred"; Mr Buchanan, who was right fast for eighteen years and then changed to slow left and did wonders with it; Mr Cobden, who took the last three Oxford wickets with consecutive balls and won the university match by two runs; Mr Booth, who in 1865 hit a ball over the Pavilion and having " 'ands like a 'ip-bath" made a catch which none who saw has ever forgotten; and, finally, "W. G." himself, who made his first appearance at Lord's in 1864 when sixteen, and scored 50, and in 1899 was elected a life member of the Club.

These are matured heroes. Then there are also great Public School figures, such as Lord Byron, cricketer and cricket epigrammatist; John Harding of Eton, who named his bat after Mrs Keate; Charles Wordsworth, afterwards the bishop, who gave Henry Manning, afterwards the cardinal, a bat and received a poetical reply containing these lines:—

> *And if there's anything on earth can mend*
> *My wretched play, it is that piece of wood;*

Picky Powell, an Eton hanger-on, who dared to say to a Harrow pugilist, "All the good I see in 'Arrow is that you can see Eton from it"; and Lord D——, who could not stand the anxiety of a close finish, but hired a cabman to drive him two miles from Lord's and then back, and on learning that Eton had won, drove all the way down Portland Place and Regent Street cheering at the top of his voice.

Such are some of the great deeds and great characters that Lord's has known, but the greatest figure was W. G. Grace. Cricket and W. G. were indeed one. Popular superstitition and the reporters had it that he was a physician, and it is true that, when a wicket-keeper smashed his thumb or a bumping ball flew into a batsman's face, first aid would be administered in the grateful shade of the "Doctor's" beard; but it was impossible really to think seriously of his medical activities, or indeed of any of his activities off the field. Between September and May one thought of him as hibernating in a cave, returning to life with renewed vigour with the opening of the season, his beard a little more imposing, his proportions a little more gigantic; so that each year the bat in his hand, as he walked to the wicket with that curious tumbling gait, seemed a more trifling implement.

With the mind's vision one sees him in many postures. At the wicket: waiting, striking and running; and again bowling, in his large round action, coming in from the leg, with a man on the leg boundary a little finer than square, to catch the youngsters who lunged at the widish ball (his "bread-and-butter trick", W. G. called it). One sees him thus and thus, and even retiring to the pavilion, either triumphantly—with not, of course, a sufficient but an adequate score to his credit—or with head bent pondering how it was he let that happen and forewarning himself against it next time. But to these reminiscent eyes the most familiar and characteristic attitude of all is W. G. among his men at the fall of a wicket, when they would cluster round to discuss the event and, no matter how tall they were, W. G.'s beard and shoulders would top the lot. Brave days for ever gone!

Of late years, since his retirement, the Old Man, as he was best known among his fellow-amateurs, was an occasional figure at Lord's. More than a figure, a landmark, for he grew vaster steadily, more massive, more monumental. What must it have been like to have that Atlas back and those shoulders in front of one in the theatre! At the big matches he would be seen on one of the lower seats of the pavilion with a friend on either side, watching and commenting. But the part of oracle sat very lightly upon him; he was ever a man of action rather than of words; shrewd and sagacious enough, but without rhetoric. That his mind worked with Ulysses-like acuteness every other captain had reason to know; his tactics were superb. But he donned and doffed them with his flannels. In ordinary life he was content to be an ordinary man.

Although sixty-seven, he did not exactly look old; he merely looked older than he had been, or than any such performer should be permitted to be. There should be a dispensation for such masters, by which W. G. with his bat, and John Roberts with his cue, and Cinquevalli with his juggling implements, would be rendered immune from Anno Domini. Almost to the end he kept himself fit, either with local matches, where latterly he gave away more runs in the field than he hit up, not being able to "get down" to the ball, or with golf or beagling. But the great beard grew steadily more grizzled and the ponderous foot-falls more weighty. Indeed, towards the last he might almost have been a work by Mestrovic, so colossal and cosmic were his lines.

London Revisited.   1926

CRICKET AND THE BACKWARD LOOK

I HAVE lately been reading again several very delightful books on cricket—Nyren's and Mr Pycroft's, Caffyn's *Seventy-one Not Out*, the Bishop of Tasmania's *History of Kennington*, Mr Pullin's *Talks with old English Cricketers*, and Albert Knight's new psychological study of the game, so patient and sincere and admirable in spirit; and though I have been very happy loitering among their pages, I have been unhappy too. Regrets will come stealing in—regrets for a day when matches were fewer, and innings were shorter and smaller and yet more glorious, and cricketers were simpler, and pitches were less perfect, and Lord's was not like a race meeting, and a hundred was called a hundred and not a century, and there was no county championship, and no evening paper *réclame*, and W. G. played for Gloucestershire, and the interval for tea (tea!) was unknown. Think of Alfred Mynn taking an interval for tea, and think of Fuller Pilch's surprise if he should alight upon a paper which (as a paper did last week) applied the headline "A Bad Start" to the score of an innings which reached 117 for two wickets. There was a time when 117 was a decent score for a whole side. It is not difficult sometimes to wish for that time once more.

I wonder if we are ever to see single-wicket matches again. They seem to have gone for ever, with the tall hat, and the grey flannel shirt, and the leg hit; and yet there must in the old days have been as much fun and excitement at a two-hours' single-wicket match as ever is extracted now from a three-day county contest.

For it is not as though the spectacle of eleven men striving to outwit and conquer eleven others were eleven times better than the spectacle of the same struggle between one and one. Quite the reverse. And considering the modern tendency to get at the essence of the thing, to take pleasures rapidly, it is rather odd that the shorter form of the game should have gone so completely out in favour of the longer. But so it is.

There are, of course, reasons enough for the decay of single-wicket. It is the highly specialised character of first-class cricket to-day that has crowded out these old genial contests between hero and hero, any balance of time left over by an early finish of a three-day match that might have been well spent in this way having now to go to the recuperation of the cricketers against their next match. Committees who have to pay their way would not like to see such wanton expenditure of strength as would be involved by a single-wicket match, or, indeed, by any of the old methods of filling up time in the interests of sport and the spectator, such as throwing the cricket ball or a hundred yards race. These are the penalties of the severity of the modern conditions of the first-class game, under which the cricketer is ceasing to be anything but a cricketing machine.

Single-wicket is, of course, a serious matter. It is a fiercer trial of all-round capacity than the ordinary game. The bowler has to bowl steadily without the rest offered by overs, and he must bat almost immediately after. Hence, considering how continuous is the strain on a county cricketer to-day, there is very good reason why it should not be played by these men in the heart of the season. But September should see many matches. The holders of the two highest averages at the end of the first-class fixtures,

D

for example, might by an unwritten law always have to meet. This would be a capital institution. The two bowlers heading the analyses might also play—probably a match of amazing brevity. But, as a matter of fact, scores in most of the historic single-wicket matches are surprisingly low, and if the old average were maintained there would be time in one day to polish off not only the two contests I have named, but perhaps one or two challenges too.

The M.C.C. ought to think seriously of a single-wicket carnival at the end of each season. It is what cricket wants, and will want still more if the present commercial and over-strenuous conditions proceed by logical progression: a touch of irresponsibility, a breath of the sporting spirit. A few merry individual challenges sandwiched in between the formal rigours and classic austerities of the inter-county fixtures would save the first-class game. The Muse of Cricket just now, I believe, has a kinder feeling for the Saturday afternooners on the village greens.

One of the more famous single-wicket matches was that at Lord's in 1810, in which Mr Osbaldeston and William Lambert backed themselves to beat Lord Frederick Beau-clerk (perhaps the greatest name in the history of cricket) and Mr Howard. Mr Osbaldeston was too ill to play, and as Lord Frederick refused to postpone the match the whole burden fell upon Lambert. Lambert was equal to the task. He made 56 and 24, and put out the others for 24 and 42. Beldham, who was there, told Mr Pycroft that Mr Osbaldeston's mother sat by in her carriage, and when the game was won called Lambert to her. After a brief interval he bore away a paper parcel, but whether it contained a gold watch or bank-notes no one ever knew. Lambert seems to have lived for cricket. One of his cousins—an old lady of eighty and a neighbour of mine—told me that he thought nothing of walking twenty-five miles to London to get a little good practice. He took the game very seriously right to the end. One night, she told me, he astonished her household—she then lived at Westerham—by walking in unexpectedly at a late hour with a thunder-cloud on his broad brow. He had been playing in a match at Tonbridge, and had been "cheated out". That was his story. To offer supper or a bed was useless. With the refrain "cheated out" on his lips he strode forth again on his way to Nutfield. Had Lambert been a boy this incident would be nothing; but he was over sixty! "And", added his cousin, "as active as a cat."

I heard the other day, between the innings of a village match, the best single-wicket story of recent times that has come my way. Two octogenarians, A. and B., both old Blues, were so carried away by enthusiasm at the last University match that they arranged a single-wicket contest. On the day appointed they met, among a number of sympathetic friends. B. won the toss, and went in and had made 12 before he was bowled; but when the time came for A. to take the bat he was unable to do so. *Anno Domini* asserted itself: his weariness and weakness were too serious; he could only lie on a sofa and cry for his lost strength. It was therefore decided that B. should go out to bowl the absent man's wicket down. Off he went, with the crowd, while A. groaned indoors in an agony of disappointment and feebleness. Suddenly, however, his friends came running back, all excitement and satisfaction. "Bravo! well played, old man!" they cried. "You've won the match —he's bowled 13 wides! "

Seriously, the revival of single-wicket matches ought to be considered, or something done to rejuvenate the first-class game. The mischief is the necessity for each county to be a going concern. Money has done the evil. When money comes in at the door joyousness flies out of the window, and first-class cricket has become a little care-worn. Some people have said that literature requires patrons, but cricket needs them far more. Cricket should be the hobby of the House of Lords, the hereditary foes to gate money. If peers had grounds and elevens there would be fun in the first-class field once more, and single-wicket matches in plenty.

À propos of patrons, I wonder how many people know that George IV was a cricketer. Albert Knight gives him due credit, and so does an earlier and less scientific writer—Peter Parley, friend of our grandfathers' boyhood. I found Peter Parley's evidence in his *Annual* for 1840; and as any story to the credit of George the Fourth is desirable, however untrue, I am pleased to bring it forward. It has two merits: it shows the First Gentleman in Europe in a light more or less gentlemanly and sportsmanlike, and it shows the national game basking (as it should, but for too long has not) in the smiles of royal patronage.

This is the story, told with a naïveté possible only to one who himself had never handled bat or ball: a naïveté which is perhaps unequalled by those who write with equal ignorance of any other subject:

"Cricket is a noble game. Why, do you know that even blood royal has stood, bat in hand, surrounded by the young buds of nobility; and I can tell you this, that the Prince of Wales, afterwards George the Fourth, was a noble cricketer, and few could bowl him out. I will tell you an anecdote of Prince George, which occurred when he was a cricketer.

"I said few could bowl him out. There was, however, a little shoemaker who lived at Slough, near Windsor; a little man, who, having a keen eye and strong arm, had acquired such extraordinary skill in bowling that few could defend a wicket against him. The Prince heard of the little man and felt desirous of trying his skill, for the Prince considered himself one of the first batsmen in the kingdom.

"A confidential friend of the Prince arranged a match between the Buckinghamshire and Berkshire cricketers, to take place on a certain day, and the Prince went disguised as a civilian.

"Well, the game began, and the Berkshire men had the first innings. The Prince being on this side, it soon fell to his Royal Highness to take the bat. 'What bit of a thing is that at the wicket?' said the cobbler.

" 'Oh, he is a tailor,' said someone who stood by.

" 'Then,' said the bowler, 'I'll break his bat for him.'

"He took his run and aim, and sent the ball with amazing force and velocity. The Prince blocked it as dead as a stone.

"The shoemaker held his hands over his eyes and surveyed the Prince from top to bottom. 'No tailor could do that,' said he; 'he must be a lad of wax.'

" 'He is,' said the second.

" 'Then I will melt him before I have done with him. Play.'

"Away went the ball again, as if it had been sent from one of the ancient war-engines.

"The Prince tipt it with the edge of his bat, without striking a blow, and it flew off to an amazing distance, in a direction by no means well guarded. Three runs was the result.

" 'You have got a *strange* customer there, I am sure,' said Long Stop, who generally stands immediately behind the wicket.

" 'We shall be better acquainted presently,' said he. 'I will give him a ball he is not used to.'

"After giving the Prince many other balls with great force, from which several runs were obtained by his clever management of the bat, the bowler seemed to summon up all his energy for one grand effort. He went back for a considerable distance, took an exact aim, ran with all his force to the popping course, and delivered—how—?

"As gently as the thistledown flies along the air; the ball ran along the grass like a snake, and stopped just in the middle of the wicket, knocking off the cross piece like a fly.

"A shout rose from the Buckinghamshire men, and the Prince threw down his bat, seemingly mortified; in a moment, however, he walked up to the bowler, and put a heavy purse into his hand.

"A horse was in waiting at a short distance, and the Prince immediately left the field. The next morning, however, the Slough shoemaker received a notice to attend the Castle. 'For,' said the Prince, 'if he makes shoes as well as he plays cricket, he shall be my shoemaker.' And this bowler was shoemaker to the Prince and George the Fourth after he came to the throne."

That is the story—which I have refrained from interrupting with the word *sic*: the triumph would have been too easy. One would perhaps wish that certain things in the match had not happened: that the Prince had retained his bat, for example, and even his purse, and that the horse had not been so ready; but the anecdote, I think, with all its faults, has great merits, if only to point the way. Our kings and princes have done so little for cricket.

But there are signs that a better time is coming. Edward the Seventh may not himself have put the scorers to much trouble or often have shed his radiance upon a great contest; but I know from personal observation that his grandsons are keen, for I saw them at the fifth Test Match at the Oval last summer, and one day at Lord's too, watching the practice. May they (to drop into the manner of Peter Parley) grow into clever managers of the bat, capable of frequently urging the ball into directions by no means well guarded!

Not only has cricket lost many of its old simplicities, it has lost its characters too. In the late process of levelling up, or levelling down, individuality has suffered. Where is our Tom Emmett to-day? Where is our bowler to bowl fifty-five wides in one year—and take a hundred wickets at fewer than ten runs apiece? Around Tom's name many good stories cluster and will ever cluster. It was Tom who warned an encroaching point: "If I were thee, mister, I'd stand a little farther back, because when I hits there I hits—hard." It was Tom who, when bowled first ball by a lob, made the classic series of answers to the commiserator in the crowd. "How was that, Tom?" "Don't Tom me." "Well, Mr Emmett, how was that?" "Don't Mr Emmett me." "Then what shall I call you?" "Call me a —— fool." Tom Emmett, after his active cricket was over, became a professional bowler at Rugby, where he stayed several years. He then coached at Leicester, and is now dead and only a memory. But he has never been commemorated rightly. Some Rugby amateur—why not Mr Norman Gale?—should make a collection of Emmettiana. Tom Emmett was the first to remark—on a bad voyage—that he thought they'd forgotten to put the heavy roller on: a joke borrowed by every seafaring cricketer since.

Pooley is another recent great name in the game. Like other cricketers before him, Pooley, who kept wicket for Surrey in the days of Southerton and Jupp, knew reverses, and became at last an inmate of a London workhouse. Says Mr Pullin, "Pooley's fists are mere lumps of deformity. Every finger on the two hands has been broken; so have the two thumbs." Jem Mace once asked to be introduced to Pooley: "Pooley," he said, "I would rather stand up against any man in England for an hour than take your place behind the wickets for five minutes." Pooley's opinion of modern cricket was not too favourable: "Why, a man ought almost to keep wicket blindfold now," he remarked after a visit to Lord's. It must be remembered that grounds in the fifties and sixties were not what they are now; and there were faster bowlers than we now have—George Freeman, for example, who once laid low all three stumps with one ball; and Harvey Fellowes, who performed the same rare feat. There were probably harder hitters too, for I understand that neither Mr Jessop nor Albert Trott has quite the power of Mr C. T. Thornton. Mr Jessop's hurricane drives are, however, good enough for me. It was told of Southerton, the slow bowler, that he used to lie awake at night wondering what he should do if Mr Thornton hit the ball straight back to him. But the great cause of bumps and bruises was bad wickets. Daft once went in to bat against Platt at Lord's with a towel round his head, so fiery was the pitch. In the same over Platt had given Summers the blow on the temple to which he succumbed. But this is nothing compared with George Anderson's stories of how a covey of partridges went up from the pitch during a match, and how Fuller Pilch would come armed with a scythe.

Cricket's triumphs of mind over might are, to me, incomparably its greatest fascination. Nothing that happens in a match is so satisfying as the successful accomplishment of a bowler's manœuvre. I remember that wonderful Sussex and Cambridge University meeting in 1891 (when 1402 runs were scored) in which Mr Brann made 161 by huge hitting. There came a time in his long innings when the Light Blue chance seemed almost hopeless, so set was he and so aggressive. Change after change was tried, but in vain, until Mr Streatfield took the ball again and remodelled the field, and Mr R. N. Douglas was motioned carefully to a spot on the ropes at the edge of the bowling screen. It was a matter of a few seconds before his place was determined; but the position was, however, exact, for when from a half-volley in the first over Mr Brann made a terrific drive, the ball, after sailing up and up an immense distance, swooped into Mr Douglas's hands and was held there, the fieldsman never having moved an inch with either foot.

The sight of that flying ball nearing that motionless, intent fieldsman, and the thought of the issue at stake, made a moment of excitement as intense as anything ever experienced in the lists of Ashby-de-la-Zouche, while the knowledge that the *coup* had been planned imparted an additional thrill.

But there are manœuvres which put less strain on the onlooker, yet by their success kindle to content for half a day. One of Lohmann's overs *à l'outrance* to a timid bat—an over in which the wicket should fall at the last ball (for Lohmann was an artist with the dramatic sense)—was a sight to live for; each ball showing a little more smilingly, though not so smilingly that the wretched man forgot to be fearful, and then the fifth—the deadly fast yorker and the scattered bails. And have you seen what "W. G." called, I believe, his bread-and-butter trick, meaning thereby a device for the dismissal of young players? First, a man carefully brought round from long leg to almost square, on the ropes, and then the short-pitched ball so tempting for a square leg hit, and so hard to keep down. I once saw two colts caught out this way in two overs. Of course, it is hardly less satisfying—and indeed, if your sympathies are with the side that is in, it is more so—when the bats-

man is wily enough to detect these snares and to defeat
them.

It is odd, with all the gusto for cricket that has been
displayed among men of letters, that Nyren's book is still
unapproached. Next to it comes Mr Pycroft's, and then, I
think, Mr Pullin's *Talks with Old English Cricketers*; but
these are some distance. The one is a classic; the others are
books about cricket. The one has magic; the others have
enthusiasm.

One would go to the sagas for the nearest parallel to the
simplicity of the old Hambledonians as described by John
Nyren, a simplicity closely allied to that of the good men
and true who spilt blood in *The Story of Burnt Njal*, that
noble record of Icelandic friendships and enmities. Indeed,
Nyren's little history is as nearly a saga as we need want.
Given bats in place of battle-axes, balls for arrows, and
amicable rivalry at the game instead of the blood feud,
and the principal differences are removed. The human
nature is the same. You have the same boyish zeal, the
same might, the same comradeship, and also the same
brilliance in feats—such as Noah Mann's masterly riding
when, dashing in at practice time on his horse, he would
bend over in the saddle and pick handkerchiefs from the
sward.

To walk over the site of the old Hambledon Ground, as
I have done, with Nyren's book in hand, is to realise
something of the glory of cricket: although there are, of
course, historic scenes nearer to hand. Indeed, there is no
need to wander in the search for sacred soil farther than
Dorset Square, since whoever passes through that urban
abode passes over the place where Lord's Ground once
stood, and where once was a stone recording a drive made
by Alexander, Duke of Hamilton, in which the ball travelled

one hundred and thirty-two yards off the bat before it touched earth. When the ground was built over this mark vanished. And yet we preserve many unimportant things; we take the greatest care of Rufus Stone in the New Forest, while the Coronation Stone is kept in the Abbey itself.

Fireside and Sunshine. 1906

A HUNDRED YEARS OF TRENT BRIDGE

Cricket is a very humanising game. It appeals to the emotions of local patriotism and pride. It is eminently unselfish; the love of it never leaves us and binds all the brethren together, whatever their politics and rank may be. There is nothing like it in the sports of mankind. Everyone, however young, can try himself at it, though excellence be for the few, or perhaps not entirely for the few. At Nottingham, during the practice hour, how many wonderfully good bowlers you see, throwing off their coats and playing without even cricket shoes. How much good cricket there is in the world!

From Andrew Lang's Introduction to
Daft's *Kings of Cricket*.

ACCORDING to tradition and to Dean Hole, who was over six feet tall and used to grow the best roses, the game of cricket in Nottinghamshire was preceded by a rudimentary pastime called Dab-and-Billet, in which the striker carried a stick and the ball was a little block of wood. In his description of a triumphant innings at Dab-and-Billet, the Dean, who was of Nottinghamshire extraction and was at school at Newark, offers us one of the best lyrical passages about sport that has ever been written:

"I maintai. that there are few more blissful emotions than those which were ours when, having hit the billet with precision and with power, we heard it whizzing through the air, saw our adversary gazing at it like a retriever at a partridge which begins to tower, and started to add runs to our score. I have heard some exquisite music, Braham's *Death of Nelson*, Sims Reeves' *Tom Bowling*, Lindley on the 'cello, Paganini on the fiddle, Koenigor on the cornet, Malibran and Jenny Lind, Rubini and Mario; I have myself played some beautiful though simple airs on the flute; but I have never heard any music, home-made or foreign, so sweet as the song of the billet."

Whether Dab-and-Billet is still played, I have not ascertained, but probably so, since Knurr-and-Spell, a similar forerunner of cricket, to this day draws Yorkshire crowds. All that we need know is that the Nottinghamshire cricket which developed from it is one of the glories of the earth.

Outside the County the first important adversaries of Nottingham were Sheffield men, and their earliest matches were in 1771 and 1772. I give the names of the Nottingham men of that time in the hope that they have descendants who will recognize them and be properly proud: Huthwayte, Turner, Loughman, Coleman, Roe, Spurr, Stocks, Collishaw, Troop, Mew and Rawson.

Nottingham's first great match with Metropolitan players came in 1791, when the M.C.C., then four years old, sent a team and won. Lord William Bentinck was the captain, his place being taken, the next day, against Twenty-two of Nottingham, by Thomas Lord himself, whose name Lord's Cricket Ground will ever perpetuate; and again the M.C.C. won. The two best Nottingham men were Humphrey Hopkin, with "full-tossing balls", and Thomas Warsop, who, in the opinion of William Clarke, the most important of all Nottinghamshire men, was the best underhand bowler he ever saw.

These matches were played on the Upper Meadow, now built over and lost beneath King's Meadow Road, Kinglake Street, Rupert Street, Goodhead Street, Essex Street, Briar Street, Castleton Street, Pegg Street and Middle Furlong Road, while other matches were played "on the Forest", the turf of which still remains. Much of the Upper Meadow Land is now occupied by the Government Munition Works.

Between 1791 and 1838, when, twenty-four years after

Lord's, the Trent Bridge ground was opened and the history of the hundred years celebrated by this little book begins, the old Nottingham Club played often; but I must not diverge to follow their deeds. All I need say is that their most dangerous foe was the Sheffield champion, Tom Marsden, best known for his single-wicket matches with Alfred Mynn.

During this epoch, the records of which are slender, one date stands out like a good deed in a naughty world, and that is December 24, 1798, for it was then that the wife of a bricklayer named Clarke, living on Bunker's Hill, Nottingham, gave birth to a son, christened William, who was destined to do more for Nottinghamshire cricket than any other man.

William Clarke, who at first followed his father's trade, was as a bowler good enough to be a playing member of the Nottinghamshire eleven in 1816. Not long after this, he gave up bricklaying to become the landlord of the Bell in the Market Place, which, while he was in charge, was the headquarters of local cricket. What good evenings, I wistfully think, they must have had.

Clarke's career is unique. Normally, the professional begins to play as a colt in the late teens, proceeds to county form, has a score of years in the front of the game, and then, at what is for most of us an early age, disappears into un-applauded obscurity. But Clarke was very different. It was not until 1836, when he was thirty-seven, that he played at Lord's; he was thirty-nine when he founded Nottinghamshire cricket; it was not until 1846, when he was rising forty-eight, that he was chosen for the Players, and it was in the same year that he added the control of the All England Eleven to his other activities. For thirty years he was a terror to batsmen.

It is often said that reputation can take wickets: that a bowler has been so much written up and talked up that a funk has been established in his opponents. This, I think, was the case with Clarke. Packed with guile, and with a profound knowledge of the game and an uncanny power of discerning character, he frequently, so to speak, took wickets before he began. He could bowl either fast or slow, although it is chiefly as a slow bowler that we think of him, and, according to Caffyn, it was his fast ball which was so deadly and which often had done its work before it was delivered. Felix records that, standing at point, he could often see the new batsman's hands trembling as Clarke advanced.

This is more strange when we reflect that Clarke was an underarm bowler and almost everyone else had taken to the new style. In Clarke's favour it must be remembered that David Harris and other bowlers of Nyren's day, although they spread devastation, were bowling on downland (unprepared, except that Harris liked molehills); whereas in Clarke's time pitches had become more true. Apart from Clarke's native genius and his capacity for taking thought, the suggestion has been made that the mere fact that, in a world trained to resist round-arm, he still bowled underarm, was greatly to his advantage. Batsmen were not instructed to receive such treatment.

Mr Pycroft, writing in the early sixties, amplifies the point. Thus:

"It was perhaps fortunate for Clarke that his art was allowed to lie fallow till the old-fashioned batsmen like old Shearman and Mr Ward had passed away, and thus it came out as a novelty to men used to the short-pitched and the inaccurate, of 'no length in particular', which ever must characterize the round-arm bowling. At first Clarke took all the best batsmen in. . . . For the first time they had encountered a man with the head to see the weak point in their game, and with the hand to pitch at the very stump, and with the very length that they did not wish to have."

Again, also in *Cricketana*, Mr Pycroft wrote:

"The exact length, according to each player's deficiencies, besides varying the pace, and (which Clarke boasted he alone could do) without indicating the change by anything observable in his delivery—this alone were enough to dispose of most men, especially if we consider that Clarke had naturally a bias in his delivery: his elbow, he said, was bowed from an accident to his arm. . . . Now, a bias with underhand bowling is more effective, because more insidious, than with a high delivery; and if a man played 'fast-footed' and forward, Clarke could bowl a ball that would miss his bat [and bowl him], or take the edge for the benefit of short slip. We once remember saying: 'How do you dispose of Mr A. C.?' 'Nothing easier, sir: I bowl him three balls to make him proud of his forward play, and then with the fourth I pitch shorter, twist, and catch him at the slip.' 'The way,' said John Marshall, 'Clarke has foretold me what chance he would give me for a catch at cover, is among the marvels of the game.'

"Every cricketer knows that there is a spot between the batsman and the bowler which, when the ball pitches on it, 'causes', as Mr Felix said, 'the most indescribable sensations'. Every player knows that out of many good lengths he will have one far more perplexing than any other. Now it was this very length [Felix related to Pycroft] that Clarke most cruelly would bowl: it was this very spot on which most mercilessly he would pitch. The first ball of that sort, Clarke would soon see he [the batsman] did not like, and that he winced under the operation; and, coolly remarking: 'We shall have a *h*accident, Muster Felix, I know we shall,' he would repeat the dose, and generally with effect."

There are many good stories of Clarke. Pycroft also tells us that he once said to a batsman: "I beg your pardon, sir, but aren't you Harrow?" and on an affirmative reply he changed his field, with the remark: "Then we shan't want a man down there." "Without head work," he said, "I should be hit out of the field." "If I were to think every ball," he said, "the other side wouldn't make a run. A man is never more taken aback than when he prepares for one ball and I bowl him the contrary one." "That gentleman," he said, pointing to a batsman, "who's so fast on his feet is as good as ready money to me. If he doesn't hit, he can't score; if he does, I shall have him." "At times," he wrote in his famous treatise on the game, to which I refer later, "it's enough to make you bite your thumb to see your best balls pulled and sky-rocketed about—all luck—but you must console yourself with 'Ah, that won't last long!' "

While, before the game, says Pycroft, other players were practising, Old Clarke, with his hands behind him, would study the wicket. His eating habits were also idiosyncratic —or so I hope. When playing, he had for lunch only a bottle of soda-water and a cigar, but in the evening he ate a whole goose. On the contrary, aspiring bowlers may like to know, Alfred Shaw could not smoke a cigar at all.

Clarke, as I have said, giving up the laying of bricks, took the Bell, and it was there, in 1831, that his son Alfred, who became a very useful player for Nottinghamshire, was born, and it was there that his first wife died. A few years later he left the Bell and, having married the landlady of the inn at Trent Bridge, he moved there, and there laid out the cricket ground which, in course of time, increasing in size and importance, became known as Trent Bridge, Nottinghamshire's headquarters, where every four years the first Test Match against Australia is played. Clarke's

E

idea, which succeeded, was to attract Nottingham cricketers
away from their pitch in—or rather on—the Forest; but at
first his charge of sixpence admission was resented, the old
ground being free. However, he persisted, and we see the
result.

According to the *Nottingham Journal* and to the
Nottingham Review, both of June 1, 1838, the first match on
the new ground was on May 28 between the Forest Club
(Barker given) and South of the Trent (Clarke given),
when South of the Trent won by 105 against 60. Clarke,
who, in spite of having but one eye, was always a skilful
bat, made 17 not out and took 4 wickets.

Among players in this match was the famous Tom
Barker, who made 10 for the Forest—Barker, who, in
addition to his prowess in the field, had a great reputation
as an authority on the game. It was he whom a youthful
amateur once asked if he would ever be out if he kept his
bat in the block without moving it. "You'll be thundering
soon out, young gentleman," was the reply, "if you do
move it." Barker lived on until 1877, when he was nearly
an octogenarian. With his long clay pipe, he was a popular
figure on every ground he visited. His last appearance at
Trent Bridge was at Richard Daft's Benefit—North v.
South—in 1876, when he complained to Bob Thoms, the
umpire, of the infrequency with which the ball was now
hit out of the ground and lost.

Another player in this first Trent Bridge match was
Redgate: not, however, the famous Sam, the best fast
bowler of his time, but T. B., his brother. "No one," says
Mr Ashley-Cooper in his *Nottinghamshire Cricket and
Cricketers*, "ever mastered Sam, who was the last player to
appear at Lord's in knee-breeches and stockings. In old
age he used to be pushed to matches in a bath-chair," as

veterans should. Others who later distinguished themselves on various occasions were William Garrat, Charles
Creswell, John Johnson (a Nottingham solicitor and the
Honorary Secretary of the County Club for many years),
John Chapman and S. Forbes. There is also a "Parr", but
this was Samuel Parr, who, in 1838, was eighteen, and not
his brother, the illustrious George, who was then only
twelve. According to tradition, George's first match was
for his native village, Radcliffe-on-Trent, against Birmingham, when he was fourteen. Sam Parr, as well as George,
later played often for Clarke's All England Eleven, and
indeed some of his best services were rendered to it.
Fuller Pilch, who was the bright particular star of this
travelling team, is reported to have said of one match at
Trent Bridge, when the brothers were in the home side,
that there would be no doubt of the issue if "they could
get rid of the two Parrs". But Nottinghamshire was successful, Guy making the winning hit.

This was Joseph Guy, whose graceful style and mien
earned him the nickname of "Gentleman Guy". It was of
him that Old Clarke said: "Joe Guy, sir. All ease and
elegance, fit to play before Her Majesty in a drawing-
room." Guy was born in 1814, and when he was not playing cricket, baked. Afterwards, like so many cricketers in
those days, he took an inn—the Roebuck in Mansfield
Road.

Other Parrs were Henry, the father, who had performed
wonders for Radcliffe-on-Trent, Samuel, the uncle, and
William, another of George's brothers. There was also,
living at Radcliffe-on-Trent, Butler Parr, the maltster, a
fine Nottinghamshire cricketer in his time, whose daughter
Richard Daft married; but this Parr is no relation to the
others.

Old Clarke, a man of great organizing ability, in 1846 added to his work as the leader of the Nottingham side the formation and management of the All England Eleven. It is not in my scheme to wander from Trent Bridge, but I must record that the "A.E.E.", as it was called, consisted of cricketers drawn from the best sources, who, by travelling all over the country, spread both the knowledge of the game and stimulated an interest in it which grew and multiplied. But for the A.E.E., cricket would not be so universal a pastime as it is; but for the A.E.E., Clarke would not be so remarkable a man.

The first of the All England Eleven's matches was played on August 31, September 1 and 2, 1846, in the Hyde Park Ground at Sheffield against Twenty of Sheffield, when the Twenty won by 5 wickets. Clarke's team consisted of himself (who went in first), J. Dean of Sussex, Dorrington of Kent (who made top score in the first innings), Fuller Pilch of Norfolk and Kent, Alfred Mynn of Kent, Joseph Guy of Nottinghamshire (who caught out five), W. Martingell of Surrey and Kent, T. Sewell of Surrey and Kent, G. Butler of Nottinghamshire, the Rev. V. C. Smith of Winchester and Oxford, and W. Hillyer of Kent, who took most of the Sheffield wickets.

In *Lillywhite's* words:

"These encounters soon caused cricket to increase vastly all over England, as being the means (especially in the North) of discovering many fine players who would never have been 'brought out' had they not had an opportunity of *first* distinguishing themselves against the England Elevens in their visits to different parts. Clarke's plan was (a liberal sum being, of course, guaranteed through gate money, etc.) to take his Eleven anywhere, and to contend either against Twenty-twos, Eighteens, Sixteens, or Fourteens according to the merits of the club or district to be encountered. When the Twenty-twos were very inferior (as was often the case), two, and even four, bowlers were also given, so as to make the match more even."

After Clarke's death, the All England Eleven was managed by George Parr.

There were, of course, rivals. *Lillywhite* mentions the United England Eleven, in 1852; the United Ireland Eleven, in 1856; the new All England Eleven, in 1858—re-formed, 1861—and another New All England eleven, in 1862. Of these the most important was the United, to which there were secessions from the All England, because Old Clarke, it is understood, could be difficult.

The year 1846, by the way, was a notable one in cricket history. It not only saw the inception of the All England Eleven, but the Surrey team was then first mobilized, and the editor of *Scores and Biographies* thinks it was then that the first telegraph-board for scoring was set up at Lord's.

An All England match, says Daft in *A Cricketer's Yarns*, wherever it was played, was always a great event.

"Certainly one never sees such holiday-making and high jinks as we used to in the old All England days, especially at those matches played in small country towns. The All England match was the topic of conversation months before the event took place. Special committees were formed to get up entertainments in the evening, and when the great day arrived the excitement was often intense. I was talking to a gentleman not long ago who told me that in order to see one of these matches (he was only a boy at the time) he rose at four o'clock in the morning and walked a dozen miles or more to the place. Another old friend, a clergyman, now nearly eighty years of age, was telling me the other day of the first time he saw me play—at Loughborough. He was rector of a small country village in Leicestershire, situated about fifteen miles away from Loughborough, and as no carriages were to be had, he and some friends engaged a cart belonging to the village chimney-sweep and made the journey in this vehicle to the match and back."

In his maturity Clarke wrote some "Practical Hints on Cricket", which he assembled in the form of a letter to the Hon. Frederick Ponsonby. Many of his details are out of date, but in general his remarks are as sound as ever. It was published in *Cricket Notes* by William Bolland in 1851 and was reprinted in *The Hambledon Men*. It will convey an idea of Clarke's thoroughness if I say that the sections are entitled the Science of Bowling, on Fielding, on Match-making, Managing and Umpiring, Advice to Practice Bowlers and The Science of Batting—"Lay your bat on the top of the ball and don't pull your bat from the ground up to it. That is not Cricket. The bat was made to play the ball."

How far-sighted Old Clarke was, may be gathered by his remark, recorded by Pycroft: "I once had thought there might be a school opened for Cricket in the winter months." He died in London on August 25, 1856.

Next to Old Clarke, the greatest early influence in Nottinghamshire cricket was George Parr, sometimes called "The Lion of the North", as Willsher was "The Lion of Kent" and Lillywhite "The Nonpareil". George Parr, who was born at Radcliffe-on-Trent on May 22, 1826, played his first match for Nottinghamshire (against Leicestershire) at Trent Bridge on June 16, 1845, and he continued an active career until 1871. He is immortal by reason of his leg-hits, often out of the ground but often landing in an elm, the remains of which are still standing at Trent Bridge and will not, I trust, ever be allowed wholly to disappear. "George Parr's Tree" it is called. When George died, in 1891, and was buried at Radcliffe-on-Trent, a branch of this elm was placed on his grave.

According to Mr William Wright, George Parr's great stroke was something in the nature of a mow. But I do not see how that matters, considering that the end was achieved and the tree cleared or battered.

Among all the curious changes which have come upon cricket none is more to be regretted than the decline of hitting to leg; and it may be surprising that one of the explanations is the niceness of modern manners. It seems that while practising in the nets in a row, every batsman but the last on the left, facing the bowlers, can be so put off by his neighbour slashing at a leg ball, that the stroke has been shelved. George Parr knew no such deterrents, and I personally should like a return to the old discourtesy.

The son of a farmer, George was a big man and, away from the wicket, a very lazy one. But he was a useful bowler and a good long field, and once at Lord's he won £5 from Sir Frederick Bathurst for throwing a cricket ball 108 yards 2 feet. It would be instructive to see how far our fieldsmen can throw a cricket ball to-day; but there seem to be either no ten minutes to spare or no interest even in so brief a contest as this would involve.

After cricket, Parr liked shooting and fishing. Many stories are told of his brusqueness and ready wit, from which irony was not missing. Thus, this is his advice to young cricketers: "When you play in a match, be sure not to forget to pay a little attention to the umpire. First of all inquire after his health, then say what a fine player his father was, and, finally, present him with a brace of birds or rabbits. This will give you confidence, and you will probably do well."

Next to George Parr as an inspiration to batsmen we should put Richard Daft, who, coming later and enjoying so long a career, is thought of almost as a modern. George Parr flourished from 1845 to 1871; Daft, beginning to play for the County in 1858, went on until almost the present century, and, after his fiftieth birthday, made seventeen hundreds, one of which, 140, was made when he was fifty-nine. It is probable that of all the players of the past—by which we may mean the nineteenth century—not one (always excepting the unique and uncataloguable "W. G.") could have adapted himself more easily and naturally to the conditions of to-day.

Daft, who was born at Nottingham in 1835, and who died in 1900 and was buried near George Parr at Radcliffe-on-Trent, was not only a superb cricketer, carrying on the tradition of Joseph Guy—to play as beautifully as any monarch could desire—but he was one of the most universally admired and beloved of men. How carefully he watched his physical fitness may be learned from Mr Ashley-Cooper's description of the daily athletic exercises which he never omitted.

I have said a good deal, and shall be saying more, to maintain that in Nottinghamshire's Golden Age some of the best cricket in the world was to be found at Trent Bridge. But not only, for a while, did the County produce the best batsmen and the best bowlers, but one of the best books about the game came from Nottinghamshire too— Richard Daft's *Kings of Cricket*. I do not claim that this is a better book than Nyren's (Hampshire) or W.G.'s (Gloucestershire), but it has a character of its own and certainly ranks very highly. Next, perhaps, I should put *Seventy-one Not Out* by William Caffyn (Surrey).

Kings of Cricket, published in 1893, has an introduction

by Andrew Lang which Daft himself solicited and which is perfect of its kind. No one loved cricket more or wrote about it with more skill and charm than Lang, who might be said to have wielded his pen rather as Daft wielded his bat. As he had never seen Daft at the wicket, he could not be as personal as we should wish, but there are passages on cricket generally in which he seems to me to say everything that need be said and to say it unimprovably. Thus:

"Cricket," he writes, "is simply the most catholic and diffused, the most innocent, kindly, and manly of popular pleasures, while it has been the delight of statesmen and the relaxation of learning. There was an old Covenanting minister of the straitest sect, who had so high an opinion of curling that he said if he were to die in the afternoon, he could imagine no better way than curling of passing the morning. Surely we may say as much for cricket. Heaven (as the bishop said of the strawberry) might doubtless have devised a better diversion, but as certainly no better has been invented than that which grew up on the village greens of England."

I like to think that it was Daft who led to these words being written.

In the field Daft seems also to have been a model to young players. "At mid-off and long-leg," says Mr Ashley-Cooper, "he was seen to the greatest advantage. He covered much ground, was quick and sure in his movements, and had a long, low, swift and accurate throw-in, the wicket-keeper receiving the ball on the first bound. Many will be able to recall his energies whilst running almost on the toes of the ring and with his straw hat often blowing off—a pleasant reminiscence which, even at this distance of time, makes one experience a thrill of delight." "And had a long, low, swift and accurate throw-in, the wicket-keeper receiving the ball on the first bound"—that is the way, and we don't see too much of it nowadays.

Although Alfred Shaw was an overarm bowler and Old Clarke was underarm, Alfred Shaw may be said to have been his successor with the ball. Before him, however, came Clarke's companions, such as Sam Redgate, of whom I have spoken, J. Bickley and R. C., or Chris, Tinley, who first appeared for the County in 1846, when he was only sixteen, and, with Bickley, was famed for his fast round-arm. Both were often chosen for England and the Players, and Bickley, who died in 1866, when only forty-seven, was also, like A. O. Jones many years after, renowned as a slip. Chris Tinley, who had the unusual name of Crispin, made a remarkable change in his attack, for after bowling fast round-arms with deadliness during Old Clarke's lifetime, on the retirement of that master he took to lobs. For the A.E.E. against Eighteen of Hallam, at Sheffield in 1860, he took 8 wickets for 54 runs in the first innings, and in the second innings all the lot for 58. Against Cambridgeshire at Trent Bridge in July 1862, he took 15 wickets for 78. He once also, for England, against twenty-two of Birmingham, caught twelve men at point. But where he would field to-day, who shall say?

"Tinsley's slows," wrote the poet whom I quote again and again in this article, "are often telling, though they sometimes catch it hot." As a bat he is described in *Lilly-white*, by Haygarth, as "an artful dodger". He lived on until 1900.

Trent Bridge's greatest fast bowlers of the past were John Jackson, J. C. Shaw, Martin McIntyre, Fred Morley, Frank Shacklock and Tom Wass, and of these Jackson was in legend the fastest: "The Demon", in fact, of his day. Jackson, who is celebrated in Prowse's verses—"Jackson's pace is very fearful"—was, however, according to some critics, not the fastest bowler of all, this proud position being given to Brown of Brighton. Next to him was possibly Harvey Fellows, and in our time Stanley Christopherson. But Jackson, who was over six feet high and weighed fifteen stone, may have been faster than either. At any rate, it was of him that was first told the story of the batsman hit on the ankle, limping away, and, on being informed that he was not out, exclaiming: "No; but I'm going."

"His performances against some of the Twenty-twos," says Caffyn, "were extraordinary, and many of the players were exceedingly glad to get out and return to the Pavilion without broken bones." Jackson seemed to have been proud of his menace. "I never got 10 wickets in a first-class match," he confessed to "Old Ebor", "but I once did something as good. It was in a North v. South at Nottingham. I got 9 wickets and lamed Johnny Wisden so that he couldn't bat. That was as good as 10, eh?"

It will perhaps be looked upon as an instance of poetic justice when I say that the one-sidedness of Jackson's nose was due to an injury in the nets at Cambridge. On this occasion first-aid was at once brought from the Pavilion, in the shape of some brandy, to rub it with. But Jackson knew better than that. "I drank the brandy," he told "Old Ebor", "and then went into the Pavilion for hot water."

John Jackson, who was born in Suffolk in 1833, died at Liverpool in 1901. In addition to being known as "The Demon", he was called "Jem Crow" and, on account of always blowing his nose resoundingly after he took a wicket, "The Foghorn".

Jackson was followed by James Coupe Shaw, known as J. C. Shaw, who was also a terror in his time. Born at

Sutton-in-Ashfield in 1837, Shaw, who was no relation of Alfred, did not join the Nottinghamshire Eleven until he was twenty-eight. A fast left-hand bowler, he carried all before him for several years, not retiring until 1875. In W. G.'s early days, J. C. Shaw, or "Jimmy" Shaw as he was to the crowd, got him twice in a first over; but the Doctor became too much for him. "It ain't a bit of use my bowling good 'uns to him now," Shaw had to admit: "It's a case of I puts the ball where I pleases and he puts it where he pleases." J. C. Shaw died in 1888.

An unusual memory of Jimmy has been given me by Mr Charles Coggan, who is one of the oldest members of the Nottinghamshire County Cricket Club. In a match against Middlesex, he says, Shaw, while fielding, got such a crack on the head from the ball that he had to be removed for repairs to the Old Trent Bridge inn and there put to bed. Meanwhile, the match, proceeding, went so definitely in favour of the visitors that Daft, the Nottinghamshire captain, was in despair. How to break up a stand in which I. D. Walker was like a rock? The only man who might do it was Shaw, and he had been put out of action.

Desperate situations, however, require desperate measures, and so Jimmy was extracted by Daft from his retirement and, all bandaged up, brought into the game again. "His reception," Mr Coggan writes, "was tremendous, and it was redoubled when with his first ball he broke up the partnership."—Such is the story, but I must admit that I have not been able to obtain verification. Anyway it is "well found".

Before leaving the question of the fastest of the Nottinghamshire bowlers, I should say that Mr Shelton, whose memory goes back a long way, considers Martin McIntyre the fastest that he ever saw. He can remember Martin with two long-stops behind the wicket-keeper. Except perhaps C. J. Kortright and an occasional over from A. E. Trott, he says he has never seen anyone so fast. Martin McIntyre was one of three brothers who helped the County, but Martin, who first played for Nottinghamshire in 1868, when he was twenty-one, was the most illustrious. He went to Australia with W.G.'s team in 1873 and died in 1885.

Alfred Shaw, whom Daft called "The Emperor of Bowlers", was born at Burton Joyce in 1842, and it was "on the road at Burton Joyce" that he learned his art. He played first for Nottinghamshire in 1864, against Kent, at Trent Bridge, and in Kent's second innings took 6 wickets. Thereafter he became a tower of strength. "If I could help it," he said to "Old Ebor", "I never bowled two balls alike. Then I always bowled for my men in the field. I used, too, to try to find a batsman's weak point and then keep him there: 'stick him up', as the saying goes. . . . In my earlier days I used to lie in bed studying how to get batsmen out, and that was how I came to be able to break both ways, to cultivate the 'dropping ball' and so on. In my opinion length and variation of pace constitute the secret of successful bowling." Old Clarke revived!

Of the great Nottinghamshire players whom we are celebrating, the only two that I met personally were Alfred Shaw and William Gunn, although, after they had emigrated south, I knew both George Bean of Sussex and Walter Wright of Kent—in fact such batting as I was capable of, Wright helped to teach me when he was a coach at Hove. With the names of these two seceders must, I fear, be placed that of a far more remarkable cricketer— William Henry Lockwood—one of the greatest fast bowlers in the history of the game, who, after being tried for Nottinghamshire in 1886, joined the Surrey forces in 1889 and remained with them, a star of the first magnitude, until the end.

Alfred Shaw I used to meet when, after his Nottinghamshire days, he moved to Sussex in 1883, at the invitation of Lord Sheffield, and looked after the Sussex colts and was a highly esteemed adviser at Sheffield Park. No one with a nose shaped like Shaw's could be anything but shrewd, and his opinions were always worth taking. On one of Shaw's yachting trips with Lord Sheffield they visited Spitzbergen and a match was played on deck in the light of the Midnight Sun. Shaw had forty people against him, passengers and crew, and he bowled them all out within an hour. Yorkshire, Surrey, Lancashire, Sussex, Kent—to name only those—have had historic cricketers who performed historic feats, but none of them can boast a bowler who took forty wickets in an hour by the light of the Midnight Sun. Not even W.G. did that.

As a bowler Alfred Shaw had no superior in stamina or accuracy; but the statement which has often been made that he would back himself to pitch a ball on a shilling every time, he himself denied. Attewell, I am sure, could do so, and James Grundy, the earlier Nottinghamshire, All England United England hero, was renowned for being able to "keep on dropping 'em on a cheese-plate".

Although William, or "Dick", Attewell came much later, not joining the side until 1881, a word may be said about him here. In 1881 he was just twenty, having been born at Keyworth, in 1861. To my eyes, he was the perfect machine, and his record of maiden overs probably was unique. He died in 1927.

According to Mr Ashley-Cooper, it was probably due to Alfred Shaw that the bowling and popping creases ceased to be cut in the turf and were marked by whitewash. An earlier Nottinghamshire man, Tom Nixon, the slow bowler, has the credit of inventing cork pads, open pads, the Balista, or catapult, and cane-handles for bats. But Nottinghamshire's fertility in ideas could go farther still, for as a proof of keenness it is told of Tom Davis, a sterling bat in the middle of the last century, that once, at the end of a match during which he had missed a catch at a critical part of the game, he insisted on receiving corporal punishment for his error, and after some protest, a bat was most conscientiously and venomously applied. It was, I have discovered, Tom Davis who, having been to the Zoo, was the first to be piqued not to be able to find the "Dangerous" (rhyming in his mind to kangaroos). " 'These Animals are Dangerous', the notice said, but I couldn't get to them."

Many of Alfred Shaw's greatest feats were accomplished with Fred Morley at the other end. In fact the names of this pair became as well known as those of Beaumont and Fletcher or Fortnum and Mason. Speaking to "Old Ebor" of the condition of the stock-bowlers in his day Daft said: "In Nottinghamshire we used to have Shaw and Morley. When we needed a change we could have Morley and Shaw."

I have mentioned the similarity between Alfred Shaw's and Old Clarke's outlook. But one of the remarks attributed to Old Clarke is actually recorded also of Shaw. According to report, Clarke used to say to his companion bowler, who very often was Jackson: "I'm going to bowl from this end; you can choose which you like." A generation or so later Alfred Shaw used to say to his companion, Fred Morley, the same thing. "Well, you see," Morley relates, "Alfred always looks at the wicket and then turns to me and says: 'I'm going to bowl at this end, Fred; you can bowl at which end you like'."

Fred Morley, who was born at Sutton-in-Ashfield in 1850, joined the team in 1872, and was one of its mainstays until 1884, when he died at the early age of thirty-three. J. C. Shaw had been a bad batsman, but Morley was worse. Daft tells us that W.G., against him, used to ask, "Who wants a catch?" and when one of the fieldsmen said: "I do," he added: "Go out yonder then," and after a ball or so the catch was given. Morley, however, could not have been fully aware of this defect, for once, when he had injured his bowling hand and someone expressed the hope that it might be well enough to permit him to play in the next match, he replied cheerily: "Oh yes, I'll play. But I shan't be able to bowl." It used to be said of Morley with the bat that as he came out to the pitch the Trent Bridge horse would automatically take its place between the shafts of the roller; but I have to confess that the same tribute is applied to Wass.

Daft describes Morley's character as child-like in its simplicity; and I like the story of him informing the other members of the team with which he went to Australia in 1882, that so poor a sailor was he that he should return "by the overland route".

Morley had no successor as a fast bowler of the same calibre, but between his death and the arrival of Tom Wass in 1906, good work with the ball was done by Barnes and Flowers, and by Frank Shacklock, a fast bowler who first appeared for the County in 1886. Shacklock played for Derbyshire for two seasons, but he was true Nottingham-shire, and from 1886 supported the team until his retirement to New Zealand. He took in all 387 wickets for 18·83 runs apiece. In 1893 against Somerset at Trent Bridge, he took 4 wickets in 4 balls, and the ball with which he did it is preserved in the Pavilion here. But perhaps his greatest feat was to bowl out Surrey in the crucial match of 1892, at the Oval, when Nottinghamshire won, and in memory of this shining event everyone on the winning side was given a medal and each of the professionals twenty guineas. A red-letter day!

Tom Wass, of Sutton-in-Ashfield, that village so productive of cricketers, was born in 1873, and "in his day", says Mr Ashley-Cooper, "was the most deadly bowler in England". During his career he took more wickets for his County than any other English bowler has done: 1,679; and he once took 3 wickets in 3 balls against Essex, and 3 wickets in 4 balls against Middlesex.

The bowler at the other end during Wass's reign— his Alfred Shaw, so to speak—was Albert William Hallam, who, with his gentle pace, provided the contrast. Before settling down at Trent Bridge, Hallam, a Nottinghamshire man by birth, had played well for Leicestershire and Lancashire and had been on the staff at the Oval. But once he had found his true allegiance he was of great service to the side. His most spectacular feats, however, were for Nelson, after he had gone over to Club cricket.

Among the early Trent Bridge batsmen I have put George Parr first and Richard Daft second, while there were various exponents "near the throne", such as Grundy and Guy and William Oscroft. But the next greatest Nottinghamshire name is that of Arthur Shrewsbury. "A planet among the stars," he is called in the Badminton book on cricket, "to watch whom getting 30 runs out of a total of 80 on a difficult wicket is far more enjoyable to a skilled spectator than to see the hundreds got on A.B.C. wickets." On a perfect wicket, however, Shrewsbury is said to have been so sure of staying in, that after lunch he used to tell Kirk, the Pavilion attendant at Trent Bridge,

F

to bring him out a cup of tea at half-past four—those being the days before an interval for tea was considered a necessity for strong men. And, by the way, I should like to have heard Alfred Mynn on this subject. "My boy," he once said to Caffyn, "beef and beer are the things to play cricket on!"

Before coming seriously to Shrewsbury, I must say that there were several Oscrofts, all from Arnold and all proficient in various sports; but in this survey William is most important. He was both a fine bat and for a while Nottinghamshire's captain. Born in 1843, he began to play for the County when he was nineteen and would have continued longer had he not been a victim of acute rheumatism. His great stroke was to leg, and he once hit a ball over George Parr's Tree, a distance of one hundred and thirty-five yards. According to Daft, in his talks with "Old Ebor", Oscroft could hit a ball that broke back, "almost harder than any man I ever saw".

Arthur Shrewsbury, in style a derivative of Daft, came into the side in 1875 at the age of nineteen and continued to play until 1902. W.G. was his only superior, and even as late as 1892, when Shrewsbury was acting as coach to Warwickshire at Edgbaston, the half-sovereign which he placed on the stumps during his informative exhibition games—of half an hour's duration every day—was never won.

In order to be in form early, says Mr Ashley-Cooper, Shrewsbury, J. A. Dixon, Attewell and William Gunn used to practise during March and April in a large room at Beeston. Other cricketers, please note.

"Shrewsbury and Gunn", "Gunn and Shrewsbury": the two names are always bracketed. How many innings they played together, and how often opened, I have not computed, but theirs is still the longest Nottinghamshire partnership: 398 against Sussex at Trent Bridge in 1890.

The giant William Gunn, who died in 1921, played for his County from 1880 to 1905, and was most worthily succeeded by his nephews John Gunn, the slow bowler, and George Gunn, his brother, on occasion the best bat in the world, both of whom are hale and hearty citizens of Nottinghamshire at this moment. John Gunn, born at Hucknall Torkard in 1876, was a deadly slow bowler and a formidable bat, who not only intimidated the foe at the wickets but was a marvel at cover-point. Altogether for Nottinghamshire between 1896 and 1925 he made 23,594 runs and took 1,150 wickets. "On ground which helped him he was unplayable"—could there be a better summer than that?

George Gunn, born at Hucknall Torkard in 1879, who I used to think batted more like an amateur than many, or even most, of that classification, supported Nottinghamshire from 1902 to 1932, and made altogether 31,842 runs, the greatest number reached by any Nottinghamshire cricketer. He is the only batsman I have seen who carried his fancies to the wicket and indulged them there. Ordinary batsmen are true to type, but George, as the fit took him, would be sometimes a hitter, sometimes a stone-waller, sometimes pure virtuoso, when his bat became a wizard's wand, and sometimes, as one of the umpires said, he would go to sleep.

On his fiftieth birthday, in 1929, George Gunn made 164 not out against Worcestershire. His son, G. V. Gunn, who was born in 1905, represents the third generation to hold this feared and honoured name.

Shrewsbury was a man of ordinary height, but William Gunn measured six feet three inches. Why either Gunn or

Shrewsbury should ever get out was a mystery, for Gunn was so tall that he could reach and smother every length ball, and Shrewsbury's defence was complete. On occasion, however, Gunn could be disdainful—a defect of his superb quality—and it was when he was in this mood that, at Hove, I once saw him bowled by an insidious lob from Walter Humphreys which he had made no effort to play at all, but which broke amazingly in and took his wicket round his contemptuous legs.

It is pleasant for a Sussex man to recall this story; because of all victims of Nottinghamshire, none provided them with so many conquests and so many runs as Sussex. The Hove ground, indeed, was so consistently fruitful to Shrewsbury and Gunn that it used to be said that if Notts won the toss, all except the first four players felt free to go down to the sea to bathe. If, however, before the arrival of Gunn to open the innings, Shrewsbury's partner had been Scotton, the bathing party might have lasted longer, for Scotton could be dislodgable. I can remember finding him very wearisome; but I am sure he would not have been played without a sound reason. At Trent Bridge in 1885 he was batting, or blocking, for an hour against Gloucestershire without scoring: against Kent in 1890, at the end of two hours he was 6 not out. On occasion, however, Scotton could hit, and he once drove a ball on to the Trent Bridge Pavilion, a distance of ninety-seven yards. But the biggest Trent Bridge hit of recent days was a stroke by F. Barratt, over George Parr's elm, which may have been longer than any of George's, since, in his day, the wickets were nearer the west side of the pitch. To hit a sixer out of the ground is a splendid thing, but I like to think of the ball crashing among these immemorial branches and the leaves falling after it.

In the modern game there is not much call for either a Scotton or a Barlow, or an Alec Bannerman; cricket has become too quick; but they served their day. And I am not sure that anyone quite so irresponsible and merry as William Barnes would receive the warmest of welcomes; but if not, the reason would not be excessive patience. Our hard-working teams, playing or travelling continually for four months, might find this convivial creature not quite serious enough. But what fun he was, and how carefree were his innings! And how destructively he could bowl! "Averages", says Mr Ashley-Cooper, "appealed not to him at all: he played simply because he loved cricket."

Barnes, of Sutton-in-Ashfield, was born in 1852 and came into the County Eleven in 1875, the same year as Shrewsbury. Great as they both were, they could hardly have been more different—for Shrewsbury played like a classic, and Barnes like a romantic. Thinking over the innings of the past which I have seen and would see again, I believe I would recreate "Barney" at his most reckless before any other player.

With him I think always of the large rubicund features of Wilfrid Flowers, who was born at Calverton in 1856 and came into the side two years later than Barnes, in 1877: the first professional ever to take over 100 wickets and make over 1,000 runs in a season. He was also one of the best throwers-in that the game has known.

Mordecai Sherwin, the famous wicket-keeper in the great period, and as leader of the side in 1887 and 1888 the last of Nottinghamshire's professional captains, was a very notable man. Born at Kimberley in 1851, he played his first match for the County in 1876, ultimately succeeding Frederick Wild. When interviewed in that year by Captain Holden at Trent Bridge as a potential wicket-keeper, he had been asked if he was afraid. "Nowt fears me," he replied. He followed by keeping wicket for Nottingham-shire for eighteen years with a remarkable record.

The fearless stumper was not a bowler, but I was present at Lord's in 1892 when he took off his gloves and pads, and, amid intense excitement, won the match against Middlesex by lobbing A. J. Webbe.

Mordecai (and I think that Sherwin must have been the only cricketer with this name) was a rotund man of mirthful character and a leading member of the Nottingham Glee Club, which used to meet at the Black Boy to sing and be hearty together. William Gunn, who was a glee singer too, lifted his voice also in the choir of St Thomas's Church.

Sherwin was the most illustrious of Nottinghamshire wicket-keepers, but in Charlie Brown, or "Mad Charlie", he had a worthy and not dissimilar early predecessor. Just, however, as Jackson's most damaging deliveries cannot be applauded, so must we deplore Charlie's trick, recorded by Daft, of removing a bail with his finger when the ball had just missed the wicket, and sending the unsuspecting batsman back to the pavilion. That was in the 1840's. To-day, umpires are more vigilant or wicket-keepers control their dexterity.

One of the most famous amateurs in the history of the game—A. O. Jones, or "Jonah"—came into the side in 1892, at the age of nearly twenty, and played until ill-health beat him in 1914. In his many first-wicket partner-ships with Iremonger, the hundred was reached twenty-four times, while his own performances were remarkable—his average for all innings during more than twenty years being 32. At third-man close in (or "gully" as he named this place) he was unique, and in addition he was a fine Rugby three-quarter and back. It is this all-round keenness that I best remember: his vigilance and his team-spirit.

Jones made the highest individual score (beating John Gunn by 2) for Nottinghamshire: 296 against Gloucestershire in 1903. His total number of catches for his County exceeds five hundred.

James Iremonger, with whom "Jonah" used to open the innings so steadily, bore the brunt of the new attack for many seasons and had a fine if not exactly a sparkling record. In 1901 he made over a hundred in four successive matches. He played for the County from 1897 to 1921 and then became a Trent Bridge coach, a post which he still adorns.

Three other stalwarts who may be honoured at this point are Joe Hardstaff, or "Hotstuff", whose nickname was so symbolical of his method, Wilfred Payton and Samuel James Staples. Payton, who was born in 1882, was, as far as can be said of anyone in this vale of uncertainty, a sure catch, as well as an aggressive defender of his wicket. Staples, twelve years younger, did not begin work for the County until 1920, but was thereafter a national figure. As for Joe Hardstaff, for many reasons he translated and humanized the phrase *Multum in Parvo*, and to-day he is not only one of the most respected of umpires but the father of perhaps the leading White Hope of England.

It was Dr G. O. Gault who took Jones's position as captain for a short while in 1914, but then came the War and a cloud fell on County Cricket which did not lift for five seasons. When the game was renewed, after, however, many tragic losses, in 1920, Mr A. W. Carr was Nottinghamshire's captain, holding the post until his retirement in 1934. One of Mr Carr's greater matches was against Sussex at Brighton in 1922, when he scored 104 out of 133 in ninety minutes, while another hard hitter, F. Barratt, was almost more disrespectful to the bowling.

Barratt, who was born in 1894 and played for Notts until 1931, was as famous for his sixers as Wellard and Tate and Gimblett have become, and at Sheffield in 1922 hit three of them in succession. Off Rhodes too! But the fiercest of all Nottinghamshire hitters was meteoric Edward Alletson, who, at Hove, in 1911, scored 189 in 90 minutes. I would have given much to be there to see; but such performances cannot be announced beforehand. "Glorious uncertainty" will always see to that.

As a rule, cricketers do not die young, or at any rate not while they are of first-class age. But there are sad exceptions, and not the least sad is the case of W. W. Whysall, who, although older than Roy Kilner (27), Colin Blythe (38) and "Jonah" (42), died at the age of forty-three. For three years Whysall had succeeded in making over 2,000 runs in the season: in 1928 having an average of over 52, and in 1929 and 1930 of over 51, and he might have been playing as long as Daft or George Gunn, had it not been for his untimely end at the close of 1930.

At the present day—our hundredth year—the team representing Nottinghamshire includes Larwood and Voce, the two fast bowlers, who stand out as pre-eminent with the ball, and Joe Hardstaff, W. W. Keeton, C. H. Harris and G. V. Gunn as the best bats. Of young Hardstaff perhaps most is expected, and I hope it may be fulfilled. He has masterly address and adventurousness, and, as I have said, he comes of the finest stock. Mr Carr, unhappily, is lost to the County, but Mr Heane is a worthy follower. Nottinghamshire has won or tied for the Championship twelve times. Last year it may have been as low down as tenth; but this year why should it not be first again?

And so we come to the end of my too brief eulogy, which, since it is concerned with the Trent Bridge ground, may fittingly conclude with praises of the Trent Bridge groundsmen who have helped towards its lustre. It has long been notorious that, in the game itself, wicket-keepers get most of the kicks and, from the commentators, very few halfpence; but groundsmen often are never mentioned at all. Yet without groundsmen where should we be? Cricket-pitches would not be what they are if it were not for the loving care which they receive from these custodians, whose solicitude is as worthy a song as that of many more exalted heroes.

The Trent Bridge groundsman of the moment is, as everybody knows, A. C. Widdowson, who, in 1935, succeeded Walter Marshall. Marshall, in course of time, had succeeded the younger "Fiddler" Walker, the younger had succeeded his father, also "Fiddler" Walker, and he had succeeded George Butler, who succeeded William Clarke, Trent Bridge's father.

The first "Fiddler" Walker, who was the first tender of the turf to apply Nottingham marl, now a universal custom all over England, had pleasant peculiarities: one of which, his manner of speaking of the pitch, has been recorded by Daft in *A Cricketer's Yarns*. Walker, he tells us, always referred to the pitch in the first person singular. Thus: "I'm better this match than ever I was. They'll never be able to wear me out; I shall be just as good on the third day as I shall be on the first." And again: "So-and-so can never get any runs except when he bats on me." That is the true spirit!

A Hundred Years of Trent Bridge. Privately Printed 1938

BOOKS AND WRITERS

A CRICKET POET

I was wondering the other day, as I watched a village game, if there is any cricketer, however normally impious, who has not, at one time or another, invoked, to quicken his eye or invigorate his arm, heavenly aid. I was not thinking then of Don Bradman or of such luminaries; but I will do so now, and, including them with cricketers of every degree down to schoolboys, express again the wonder whether they have not, at one time or another, invoked heavenly aid. I know that I did.

That such outside influences can be called upon we are aware also from printed words on the game nearly two centuries ago—earlier than we usually think of cricket as a moving spectacle at all; but as long ago as the seventeen-forties, James Dance, under his alias of James Love, an Oxford undergraduate who later played for Richmond, was writing his mock-heroic poem *Cricket* in celebration of the first match given in Lillywhite's *Scores and Biographies*, the match between Kent and Richard Newland's eleven, a match in which two at least of the contestants besought the interference of the gods: one for strength to hit and one, having hit, for the fieldsman to fail to hold. Bryan, for instance, before he hit that five, desired the Propitious Powers to assist his blow and to grant that the flying orb might shock the Foe; which it (or, in other words, the batter'd Pellet) did. But peruse the whole passage:

> *Bryan, collected for the deadly Stroke,*
> *First cast to Heav'n a supplicating Look,*
> *Then pray'd—'Propitious Pow'rs! Assist my Blow.*
> *And grant the flying Orb may shock the Foe!'*

This said; he wav'd his Bat with sourceful Swing,
And drove the batter'd Pellet o'er the Ring.
Then rapid five times cross'd the shining Plain,
E'er the departed Ball return'd again.

As I said—a five.

But here let me give in full Lillywhite's first recorded match, merely stating that it was by no means the first important one to be played. Two or three London newspapers had been giving notice of other matches, both at the Royal Artillery Ground, which still may be visited in Moorgate Street, and at Lamb's Conduit Fields, for several years. This is Lillywhite's entry:

"In 1746, Lord John F. Sackville issued a challenge on the part of the county of Kent, to play 'All England'. This match came off at the Artillery Grounds, in Bunhill Fields, Finsbury Square, London, and is recorded in the *Gentleman's Magazine* for the year. It assembled the first players from all parts, and proved a well-contested match. It may as well be premised, that the curved bat, the wide stumps (two in number), and the old system of bowling then prevailed; and that the fielding must have been *good*, or the batting *bad*, or the ground very heavy, to produce such a score under such circumstances."

Lillywhite adds that Long Robin was, as indeed we suspected, a feigned name. In a record kept in a certain Kentish pavilion, it is said tersely that he was at once one of the best cricketers and worst men in England.

We will return later to the supplicatory fieldsman, but meanwhile I should say that James Dance, the poet, was one of the sons of George Dance, the architect, first of that name. It was not, as has been stated, in the forlorn hope of bettering his fortunes that James changed his patronymic to Love, but as a compliment to his wife, whose surname was Lamour. Meanwhile his brother George, the second architect, and his uncle Nathaniel, the painter, were prospering. The Dances, indeed, seem to have been an interesting company, starting with the George Dance who designed the present Mansion House, and proceeding with his sons, whom I have mentioned, and his grandson the dramatist, also a George Dance, who died in 1863, just within living memory, and, in addition to burlesques with Planché, wrote, among certain farces which had a long life, such as *Delicate Ground* and *Naval Engagements*, a play that I should much like to glance at, called *Izaak Walton*. In these days, when men of letters and women of letters appear on the stage in the unfamiliar rôle of central characters, and even poor Rossetti's frailty has been exploited on the boards, I should like to see what could be done dramatically with the *Compleat Angler*.

George Dance the first was born in 1700. His Mansion House has solidity, and I am sure that the Lord Mayor is glad to see again its sombre and massive yet welcoming façade when he returns home from any jaunt; but personally I should prefer a Mansion House which might have been built there instead. For the story goes that a design for this important building, by no less an architect than Andrea Palladio, which, two centuries late, was put at the disposal of the authorities, would have been seriously considered had not Lord Burlington, the chairman, dismissed it as the work not only of a Papist, but of one who had not been elected a Freeman of the City. Dance, however, did reasonably well, and he designed also St Luke's, in Old Street, where he was buried.

George Dance the second, who was born in 1741, has a special interest in being one of the original forty members of that much-criticized but steadily surviving institution, the Royal Academy. To this he added the further unique distinction of outliving the others, so that when he died, in 1825, and was buried in St. Paul's Cathedral, he was, of the forty, the last. Although, for a while, the R.A.'s Professor of Architecture, Dance never lectured, and, indeed, he behaved more like an artist than an architect, contributing to the august walls a large number of portraits in chalk, which, as engraved by Daniell and published, serve historians well. His principal work, Newgate Prison, has been replaced by the Central Criminal Court.

But this Dance was not the only member of his family to be an original member of the Forty, for his brother Nathaniel was one of them as well. Other honours also came Nathaniel's way, for, failing to win the affections of Angelica Kauffmann, he married the daughter of a baronet, and himself, in due course, was created a baronet too. He also assumed the name of Holland, and entered Parliament, continuing to paint now and then; but neither he, nor his architect father, nor his architect brother, ever wrote a mock-heroic poem on cricket, or added to our knowledge of the union of proficiency and piety.

As for the poet, first James Dance and afterwards, as actor and playwright, James Love, I find that his second instance of proficiency allied to piety occurred when Newland, hitting high (as they practically always did in those days before the bat was straight), was careful to employ against the fieldsman, who happened to be Lord John Sackville, what influence he had Above. Thus, as the glancing ball (which has now become the ascending Pellet) mounted upwards in the air, he, too, had recourse to intercession.   .

The Batsman sees it; and with mournful Eyes,
Fix'd on th' ascending Pellet as it flies,

Thus suppliant claims the Favour of the Skies.
'O Mighty Jove! and all ye Pow'rs above!
Let my regarded Pray'r your Pity move!
Grant me but this. Whatever Youth shall dare
Snatch at the Prize, descending thro' the Air;
Lay him extended on the Grassy Plain,
And make his bold, ambitious Effort vain.'

Meanwhile, I take it, Lord John's supplication was directed wholly to making the catch; and in the result, I must add, his prayer was successful, although half of Newland's was gratified, for in making the catch Sackville fell.

The match eventually was won by Kent, the critical moment coming when Waymark—

Waymark was ready; Waymark, all must own,
As sure a swain to catch as e'er was known—

dropped the ball.

The assumption is that Waymark had not sufficiently placated the gods. That modern fieldsmen also are not incapable of piety, I have a further proof in the reminiscence sent me by an old Eton master. The batsman in was C. I. (or Buns) Thornton, no less, and the fieldsman was standing "very deep long-on almost in the left-hand corner under the trees as you look from the Slough Road. Before long there was a terrific skier and several appeared to be run while the ball was in the air". But the catch was made. When the fieldsman was asked, afterwards, what he did while he was waiting, he replied, "I prayed to the Lord."

Another correspondent tells me that it is not only cricketers who resort to Divine intervention. Exactly the same anxious appeal, he says, was made in Matthew Concanen's mock-heroic poem, *A Match at Football*, in 1721.

Whether such prayers are quite playing the incom-

G

parable game, the casuist (and the Committee of the M.C.C.) must decide; yet since both teams have recourse to entreaty (and, in my opinion, always have had and always will), there is not much to be said, in the Chair or out of it.

Only the Other Day.   1936

JOHN NYREN

It is due in great part to John Nyren's humility, which places him in his books a little lower than any of the good fellows who batted and bowled for the old Hambledon Club, that the erroneous impression is abroad that the author of the noble pages of *The Cricketers of My Time* was an illiterate rustic, incapable of writing his own memories.

I do not suggest that every one is so mistaken; but too many people who have read or have heard of Nyren seem to entertain this view. Again and again in conversation I have had to try to put the matter right, although it needs but a little thought to realize that only very fine qualities of head and heart—only a very rare and true gentleman-liness—could have produced the record of such notable worth and independence and sterling character as shine in that book. Good literature is no accident; before it can be, whether it is the result of conversations or penmanship, there must have been the needful qualities, as surely as the egg precedes the chicken. I do not mean that it is not in the power of an illiterate rustic to talk greatly; but it is not in the power of one who remains an illiterate rustic to talk such great talk as *The Cricketers of My Time*.

A fortunate error in an article on John Nyren, which I wrote five years ago, brought me acquainted with Miss Mary Nyren and her sisters—John Nyren's grand-daughters—now living at Folkestone; and Miss Nyren was so good as to write out for me a little paper of memories of her grandfather, collected from various family sources, which carry the story of his life a little farther than Mr J. W. Allen's excellent memoir in the *Dictionary of National*

Biography. In Miss Nyren's notes, as well as in that article, John Nyren—to whom cricket was, as it ought to be, only a recreation—stands forth a Roman Catholic gentleman of cultivated tastes, a good musician, a natural philanthropist, and the friend of very intelligent men, among them Charles Lamb's friends Leigh Hunt, Cowden Clarke, and Vincent Novello. These things were always known to the few; they ought to be known also to the many.

John Nyren was born at Hambledon on December 15, 1764. His education, says his granddaughter, was desultory, largely owing to the difficulties then inseparable from his religion. We must suppose that as a boy he helped his father in various ways on his farm. He joined the Hambledon Club in 1778, when he was fourteen, as 'a farmer's pony'; he stood by it until 1791, when his father moved to London and the great days were over. Only a few reports of the matches remain, owing to the fire of which I have spoken. Lillywhite, in the *Cricket Scores and Biographies*, gives in the great Richard-Nyrenic period but four in which John Nyren's name appears (and in two of these the name may be that of Richard, and not John). The first of them was in June, 1787, on the Vine at Sevenoaks (where I watch good matches every summer), between the Hambledon Club (with Lumpy) and Kent. Kent won by four wickets, and Nyren (J. or R.) made 10 and 2. Noah Mann was run out, 0, in both innings—the impetuous gipsy! Tom Walker made 43 and 10, and H. Walker 39 and 24. In July, on Perriam Downs, near Luggershall, in Wiltshire, Nyren (J. or R.) played for Mr Assheton Smith against the Earl of Winchilsea, and made 2 and 2. For the Earl, Beldham made 30 and 22, and David Harris took ten wickets, including Nyren's. In the match England *v.*

Hambledon, on Windmill Down, in September, 1787, J. Nyren (J. this time) made 3 and 1; and for Hampshire against Surrey, at Moulsey Hurst, in June, 1788, he made 3 and 9, and was bowled by Lumpy both times.

And here the name drops out of Lillywhite until 1801, when John was thirty-six and established in London in business. Thenceforward it occurs many times in important matches, until his last match in 1817. To these games I come later, merely remarking here that Nyren's new club was the Homerton Club, then the most famous next to the M.C.C. About 1812 it moved from Homerton to the new Lord's ground, amalgamating with the St John's Wood Club, and afterwards with the M.C.C. itself.

John Nyren married in 1791, the year of Richard Nyren's departure from Hambledon. His bride, Miss Nyren writes, was—

"Cleopha Copp, a wealthy girl not quite seventeen, of German parentage, highly educated, and wonderfully energetic. Three days after the birth of her first child, at Portsea, she got up and went downstairs to interpret for some French priests who had emigrated from France owing to the Revolution—there being no one else who could speak to them in French. Her mother, Mrs Copp, was a pioneer of work in the East End of London; she took a large house at West Ham at her own expense, and gave fifty young French female refugees employment in lace making, chiefly tambour work; employing a Jesuit priest to give them instruction two or three times a week."

Until 1796 John Nyren, whose wife had provided him with a competency, lived at Portsea; in that year he moved to Bromley, in Middlesex; later to Battersea; then to Chelsea, where he had a house in Cheyne Walk; and finally to Bromley again, where he died.

Nyren played in his last important match when he was in his fifty-third year. I regret to say that he did not trouble the scorers. He played for Lord Frederick Beauclerk's side against Mr William Ward's side, at Lord's, June 18, 19, and 20, 1817. Thumwood bowled him. For Mr Ward (to whom Nyren dedicated his book) Lambert made 78 and 30 and Beldham 4 and 43. Lord Frederick made 28 and 37, and Mr Osbaldeston 10 and 39 not out. Lord Frederick won by six wickets.

To the score of this match Mr Haygarth appends an account of Nyren:

"He was an enthusiastic admirer of the 'Noble Game' ('his chivalry was cricket'), and about 1833, published the [Young] Cricketer's Guide [Tutor], a book which contains an account of the once far-famed Hambledon Club, in Hampshire, when it was in its prime and able to contend against All England. Had not this book (which, however, is sadly wanting in dates, especially as to the formation and dissolution of the club, etc.) appeared, but little would now be known of those famous villagers.

"Nyren was left-handed, both as a batsman and field, and played in a few of the great matches at Lord's after leaving his native village, being for several seasons a member of the Homerton Club. Considering, however, that he continued the game till he was past sixty, his name will but seldom be found in these pages. It does not appear at all from 1788 to 1801, or from 1808 up to the present match. He was a very fine field at point or middle wicket, was 6 ft. high, being big-boned, and of large proportions."

Among the very few persons now living that remember John Nyren is Canon Benham, who as a boy once met him. Canon Benham tells me that a story illustrating Nyren's judgment in the field used to be told, in which that player calculated so accurately the fall of a ball hit high over his head that, instead of running backwards to it in the ordinary way, keeping his eye on it all the time, he ran forwards and then turned at the right moment and caught it. Canon Benham also recalls a great story of a Hambledon match at Southsea. When the time came for Hambledon's second innings, six runs only were wanted. The first ball, therefore, the batsman—whose name, I regret, is lost—hit clean out of the ground into the sea, and the match was won. Canon Benham can remember the striker's tones as he corroborated the incident: "Yes, I sent hurr to say."

I now resume Miss Nyren's narrative:

"My grandfather was enthusiastic about cricket and all that concerned it to the last day of his life, but only as a pastime and recreation, not as an occupation, as writers of the day would make out. I will quote *en passant* a passage written by his eldest son, Henry. 'My father, John Nyren, was known to the crickets of his time at the Marylebone Club as "young Hambledon". He was a constant player of that manly game, and excelled in all its points, generally carrying out his bat, often keeping the bat two whole days, and once three. [This would be, I assume, in minor matches.] When fielding, by the quickness of his smart, deep-set eyes, he would catch out at the point; this was his favourite feat, and his fingers carried the marks of it to his grave. With some batters one might as soon catch a cannon-ball.'

"My grandfather could use his left hand as dexterously as his right. He was a good musician, and a clever performer on the violin, an intimate friend of Vincent Novello's, and a constant attendant at the celebrated 'Sunday Evenings' at his house. There he met Charles Lamb, Leigh Hunt, Cowden Clarke, Malibran, and other celebrities. He often took with him his youngest son, John William Nyren, my father, then a lad, who in later years often told me and my sisters how he enjoyed listening to the witty conversation and the good music which always formed part of the entertainment."

That Nyren loved music is very clear to the reader of *The Cricketers of My Time*. He says, it will be remembered, of Lear and Sueter's glees at the Bat and Ball, on Broad-Halfpenny:

> *I have been there, and still would go;*
> *'Twas like a little heaven below.*

It is interesting to note that Charles Lamb uses the same quotation from Dr Watts in his account of the musical evenings at Novello's.

Both Leigh Hunt and Cowden Clarke, as we shall see, have written of their friend; but I cannot find any reference to him in the writings of Charles Lamb. I wish I could, for Lamb, although he would have cared even less for cricket than for music, would have been one of the first to detect the excellences of Nyren's book, especially such passages as the robustly lyrical praise of ale, and the simple yet almost Homeric testimony to the virtues of the old players and celebration of their unflinching independence.

Miss Nyren continues:

"My grandfather was very fond of all children, and much beloved by all Vincent Novello's family: they called him 'Papa Nyren'. One of the daughters, the late Mary Sabilla Novello, wrote as recently as 1903, that she well remembered him when she was very young, as being 'very kind and indulgent to little children, always ready to join heartily in all their merriments'. We still have heaps of music inscribed to him by Vincent Novello, with all kinds of playful and affectionate words. It was my grandfather

who first remarked the beauty of Clara Novello's voice, and
advised her father to have it carefully trained. He composed
three pieces of music which Novello published, two of
which were 'Ave Verum' and the accompaniment to
Byron's spirited song 'Fill the Goblet again'; I do not
know what the third was."

Miss Nyren continues:

"He was himself a temperate man, though he wrote the
music for this convivial song and a panegyric on 'good
strong ale'. He was quite as enthusiastic about music as
cricket, and in his old age much enjoyed reading over the
score of Novello's masses and other music, saying he could
imagine he heard the sound of each instrument.

"For thirteen years he was honorary conductor or choir
master of the choir of St Mary's, Moorfields, where Novello
was organist, and five years after his death the choir sang,
on June 26, 1842, in memory of him his own 'Ave Verum',
with chorus. Vincent Novello was at the organ, and Miss
Dolby and Miss Lucumbe and Gamballi were the solo
singers.

"He was an exceptionally strong man, as the following
anecdote will prove. My father well remembered going
with his father to see some great boxing contest, where
there was a great crowd, and John Nyren senior felt a
hand in his coat pocket; he quickly caught it by the wrist
and firmly held it, lifting the culprit, a boy, up by it for
the crowd to see, and then let him go, thinking him
sufficiently punished.

"In one of my grandfather's visits to Belgium an archery
fête was in progress. He had never handled a bow, but on
being asked to try his skill, did so, and his correct eye and
steady hand enabled him to place the arrow exactly in the
centre of the bull's-eye. He was asked to shoot again; but
he courteously declined, simply saying: 'I have shown you
what I can do.' Simply; but shrewdly too, I guess.

"John Nyren was never a good man of business, being

too kind in helping others to enrich himself. He was a
calico printer on a large scale, but his premises were burnt
down, and he lost a great deal of property. He and his wife
were always ready to help those in trouble of any kind,
and those who had the privilege of knowing them have
told me how all their friends, and even acquaintances, when
in sorrow or any difficulty, always went to consult 'old
Mr and Mrs Nyren', their sympathy and advice being much
valued, especially by young people.

"Their family consisted of two sons and five daughters;
two others died young. The eldest son, Henry, never
married; the youngest son, John William, only did so some
years after his father's death, and left three daughters—still
living. His little son, the only grandson of John Nyren,
who bore his name, died young, and was buried close to his
grandfather. Three of John Nyren's daughters married,
and have left many descendants, but none named Nyren.
One of his daughters became Lady Abbess of the English
convent at Bruges.

"My grandfather was very fond of all animals, but more
especially dogs; he generally had one or two about him.
He was once bitten by a mad one, but happily no bad results
ensued, though it was reported he had died from the effects.
It is a rather curious fact that the Duke of Richmond, who
afterwards died from the bite of a tame fox, and who had a
great dread of hydrophobia, while strolling about Lord's
cricket ground several times asked my grandfather about
this very unpleasant experience; asking many questions and
taking much interest in all the details.

"John Nyren was very partial to the little black Kentish
cherry, and for many years one of his 'noble playmates' sent
him annually a hamper full of them, which he always
received with boyish pleasure, at once opening it himself
and enjoying the fruit with his family and any children who
happened to be with him.

"There is no doubt John Nyren himself wrote *The Young
Cricketer's Tutor* and *Cricketers of My Time*; Cowden
Clarke only edited them. It was Cowden Clarke who

suggested that he should write and print his cricketing recollections, and very much amused and astonished the old gentleman by the idea."

Here Miss Nyren's manuscript ends, bringing us to controversial ground. Nyren's title-page describes Cowden Clarke as the editor, and Clarke's account of the making of the book is that it was "compiled from unconnected scraps and reminiscences during conversations". In other words, Clarke acted as a reasonably enfranchised stenographer. Mrs Cowden Clarke, in *My Long Life*, says something of her husband's share in Nyren's book, referring to Nyren as "a vigorous old friend who had been a famous cricketer in his youth and early manhood, and who, in his advanced age, used to come and communicate his cricketing expressions to Charles with chuckling pride and complacent reminiscence". One thing is certain and that is that Clarke, who wrote much in the course of his life, never wrote half so well again as for Nyren; and this is an important piece of evidence in favour of his duties being chiefly the reproduction of the old cricketer's racy talk. I have seen, I think in the *Tatler*, Leigh Hunt's paper, an original description of a match by Cowden Clarke, which contains no suggestion of the spirit of the *Tutor*. At the same time, I must confess that the little sketch of a cricket festivity from John Nyren's unaided hand, which I quote below, is also so unlike the *Tutor* as to cause us to wish that Cowden Clarke had been reporting his friend then also. Neither man did such spirited work alone as when the two were together.

The best account of John Nyren is that which Cowden Clarke wrote for the second edition of their book, in 1840, after Nyren's death, beginning thus:

"Since the publication of the First Edition of this little work, the amiable Father of it has been gathered to the eternal society of all good men."

Cowden Clarke continues:

"My old friend was a 'good Catholic'—'good,' I mean, in the mercantile acceptation of the term—a 'warm Catholic'; and 'good' in the true sense of the word I declare he was; for a more single- and gentle-hearted, and yet thoroughly manly man I never knew; one more forbearing towards the failings of others, more unobtrusively steady in his own principles, more cheerfully pious; more free from cant and humbug of every description.

"He possessed an instinctive admiration of everything good and tasteful, both in nature and art. He was fond of flowers, and music, and pictures; and he rarely came to visit us without bringing with him a choice specimen of a blossom, or some other natural production; or a manuscript copy of an air which had given him pleasure. And so, hand in hand with these simple delights, he went on to the last, walking round his garden on the morning of his death.

"Mr Nyren was a remarkably well-grown man, standing nearly 6 ft, of large proportions throughout, big-boned, strong, and active. He had a bald, bullet head, a prominent forehead, small features, and little deeply sunken eyes. His smile was as sincere as an infant's. If there were any deception in him, Nature herself was to blame in giving him those insignificant, shrouded eyes. They made no *show* of observation, but they were perfect ministers to their master. Not a thing, not a motion escaped them in a company, however numerous. Here was one secret of his eminence as a Cricketer. I never remember to have seen him play; but I have heard his batting, and fielding at the point, highly commended. He scarcely ever spoke of himself, and this modesty will be observed throughout his little Book. He had not a spark of envy; and, like all men of real talent, he always spoke in terms of honest admiration of the merits of others."

Leigh Hunt wrote thus, when reviewing *The Young Cricketer's Tutor* ("Messrs. Clarke and Nyren's pleasant little relishing book"), in the *London Journal* for May 21, 1834:

"It is a pity the reader cannot have the pleasure of seeing Mr Nyren, as we have had. His appearance and general manner are as eloquent a testimony to the merits of his game as any that he or his friend has put upon paper. He is still a sort of youth at seventy, hale and vigorous, and with a merry twinkle of his eye, in spite of an accident some years ago—a fall—that would have shattered most men of his age to pieces. A long innings to him in life still, and to all friends round the wicket."

It was a few weeks after this review of Nyren's book that Leigh Hunt printed in the *London Journal* a letter from the old cricketer (not so old as he had been called, however), describing a cricket festival, which is notable chiefly for the masterly way in which he avoids describing the match itself. If ever a reader was disappointed, it is surely here! It is as though Paderewski stepped to the piano and—recited a poem; or Cinquevalli, with all his juggling implements about him, delivered a lecture. But the little article has such a pleasant naïveté that we must forgive the omissions.

To the Editor of the *London Journal.*
Bromley, Middlesex,
June 25, 1834.

My Dear Sir,
The wise men of the East invited me to stand umpire at a cricket match, the married men against the bachelors. The day was highly interesting, and I cannot forbear giving you

a short account of it. If you can take anything from the
description I give you for your paper, do it any way you
like; this will be only a rough sketch. I call these gentlemen
'the wise men of the East', as they will not suffer their
names in print, and they live at the East End of London.

When we arrived at the place of our destination I was
both surprised and delighted at the beautiful scene which
lay before me. Several elegant tents, gracefully decked out
with flags and festoons of flowers, had been fitted up for the
convenience of the ladies; and many of these, very many,
were elegant and beautiful women. *I am not* seventy; and
'the power of beauty I remember yet'. I am *only* sixty-
eight! Seats were placed beneath the wide-spreading oaks,
so as to form groups in the shade. Beyond these were
targets for ladies, *who love archery*, the cricket ground in
front.

The carriages poured in rapidly, and each party as they
entered the ground was received with loud cheers by such
of their friends as had arrived before them. At this time a
band of music entered the ground, and I could perceive the
ladies' feathers gracefully waving to the music, and quite
ready for dancing. However, the band gave us that fine
old tune 'The Roast Beef of Old England'.

We entered a large booth, which accommodated all our
party; a hundred and thirty sat down to the *déjeuner*. Our
chairman was *young*, but old in experience. Many excellent
speeches were made; and ever and anon the whole place
rang with applause. After this the dancing commenced—
quadrilles, gallopade, etc., etc. It was, without exception,
the most splendid sight that I ever witnessed, and re-
minded one far more of the descriptions we read of fairy-
land than of any scene in real life. The dancing was kept
up with great spirit, till the dew of heaven softly descended
on the bosoms of our fair countrywomen.

Not a single unfortunate occurrence happened to damp
the pleasure of this delightful party. Had you been with us
you would have sung 'Oh, the Pleasures of the Plains', etc.,
etc. How is it that we have so few of these parties? Can

any party in a house compare with it? God bless you and yours.

JOHN NYREN.

P.S.—The cricket match was well contested, the bachelors winning by three runs only.[1]

Nyren's book (of which the present [in *The Hambledon Men*] is the fourth modern reprint[2]) stands alone in English literature. It had no predecessor; it has had no successor. The only piece of writing that I can find worthy to place beside it is Hazlitt's description of Cavanagh, the fives player, which is full of gusto—the gusto that comes of admiration and love. There is no other way—one must keep to one's friends; the inter-county game and its players have grown too public, too commercial, for any wider treatment to be of real merit. But I doubt very much if any more really great literature will collect about the pitch. The fact that Tom Emmett was allowed to die, a year or so ago, without a single tribute worth the name being written is a very serious sign. There was a "character", if the world ever saw one; but not one of his old friends or associates, not one of his old pupils at Rugby, seems to have thought it worth while to set down any celebration of him. That seems to me very unfortunate,

---

[1] Leigh Hunt, whose attitude to his contributors and readers was always paternal, appends some notes, of which I quote one:—" 'The world!' The man of fashion means St. James's by it; the mere man of trade means the Exchange, and a good, prudent mistrust. But cricketers, and men of sense and imagination, who use all the eyes and faculties God has given them, mean His beautiful planet, gorgeous with sunset, lovely with green fields, magnificent with mountains—a great rolling energy, full of health, love, and hope, and fortitude, and endeavour. Compare this world with the others—no better than a billiard ball or a musty *plum*." [E.V.L.]

[2] The others were Messrs Sonnenschein's, Mr Ashley-Cooper's and Mr Whibley's. To Mr Whibley, I believe, belongs the honour of discovering or re-discovering the literary merits of the work. It was his praise of it in the *Scots* or *National Observer* that first sent many readers to the original.
[E.V.L.]

and very significant. In the new bustle of county champion-
ships, too many matches, and journalistic exploitation,
individuals are being lost.

John Nyren died at Bromley on June 28, 1837. He had
been living for some time, with his son, in the old royal
palace there. If the reader—the next time that he visits
South Kensington Museum—will make a point of seeing
the carved overmantel from Bromley Palace which is
preserved there, he will have before him a very tangible
memento of the old cricketing gentleman, for it was taken
from Nyren's room when the house was pulled down.

The Hambledon Men.   1907

WINTER SOLACE

By a happy chance I found myself the other day of frost in the library of a cricket enthusiast, surrounded by most of the literature of the great game, and not a little of its art. I had not much time, but I used it to some purpose, I think, turning over the leaves with an avidity quite equal to that of a connoisseur of typography, and being, perhaps, more continually rewarded, for interesting human facts are commoner than good printing, especially among that simple folk the old heroes of bat and ball. For, of course, it was to the old rather than the new that I resorted. The new are (if it were possible) almost too much with us; but the old, how far away!

Perhaps the rarest book that I handled was the tiny volume of recollections of cricket by Lord Charles Russell, of which twelve copies, and twelve only, were printed in 1879, for the members of his lordship's team at Woburn Abbey. The little brochure is only thirty-nine pages long, consisting, in its author's words, of a single over, the first ball of which was contributed—as the copy which I saw attested in his lordship's hand—by the late George Richmond, R.A., under the pseudonym of "Octogenarian".

Of what is the old man thinking
As he leans on his oaken staff?

is the motto. Of what but cricket, of course! Of what else should old men be thinking? Lord Frederick Beauclerk, W. Ward, Esq., Lillywhite (the Nonpareil), George Parr, and Lord Charles Russell himself—these were his brave thoughts. One story which he gives of old Lilly (not

H   113

Lilly the grammarian, by any means)—*the* old Lilly—is
new to me: "I suppose," he remarked to Mr Richmond,
"I suppose if I was to think every ball, they wouldn't
ever get a run." What a game to watch—old Lilly thinking
every ball! "But," he added, "three balls out of four
straight is what we calls mediogrity." Who would have
guessed that word? Lord Charles Russell, under the
alluring title *Round-arm Recollections*, has another story of
Lilly, to the effect that he often refused a hard chance of
c. and b. with the remark, as he glanced at the magical right
hand which had been drawn out of danger: "Ha! where
would you be without my bowling?"—"bowling" being
very properly pronounced by the Nonpareil to rhyme with
"fowling". This little book, by the way, is an excellent
example of what one might call gentlemen's literature,
privately printed of course. I should like a book-case of
such volumes, and, indeed, I have a few, including the
priceless record of the Allahakbarries' Eleven. There lies
before me a copy of the letter in which Lord Charles
Russell bade farewell to the active game, in 1861.

"I shall be delighted," he wrote to his son, Henry
Russell, "to coach you in cricket, but I play no more. My
last match was creditable—8 singles well but slowly got,
and bowled by a very first-rate ball. I took off my cap when
I received the applause of the Pavilion: and, as John retires
from the scene of his glory before his powers leave him, so
I take leave of cricket. Next season I shall be nearer sixty
than thirty, so Cricket society can no longer have a claim
on me."

John was Lord John Russell, who had just accepted a
peerage.

Another story of old Lilly I find in one of Frederick
Gale's genial volumes, *The Game of Cricket*: "I remember

one night"—Fuller Pilch is speaking—"when there was a
concert. Mr Felix was playing in the band, and old Lillywhite was sitting behind him and saw the music. 'Mister
Felix,' he said, 'you're bound to have an overthrow or two
among all those crooked notes.' " This book, by the way,
was presented by its author to the late Bob Thomas, best
of umpires and most sterling of independent dependants
(that fine class of men). A scrap of the old man's dignified
writing—for Bob wrote a good self-conscious letter—was
in it, sent, evidently, with the book to a friend and returned
by accident in its pages:

> The "Old Buffer's" book I think will please you;
> which can be returned, when its contents have been
> leisurely scanned; and digested.
> Truly yours,   Rob. Thoms.

Felix was not only the perfect bat of his day, but an
author on the game too; for it is a mistake to think that it is
a new thing for great cricketers to write about their art.
On the contrary, they always did it a little: Lambert in
1816, Nyren in 1833, Felix in 1845, and Old Clarke (in
William Bolland's book *Cricket Notes*) in 1851. Lambert's
book, you observe, was the earliest. This was the same
William Lambert of whose cousin I wrote in the essay on
George Mariner. What share he had in his *Instructions and
Rules for Playing the Noble Game of Cricket* I know not;
but he confesses to help from his publisher. The result is
lacking in character, and is chiefly interesting for the
frontispiece, depicting a match at Lewes, in Sussex.
Publishers and authors are not ideal collaborators; the
lion does not easily and naturally lie down with the lamb,
except, as the old wit said, with the lamb inside. Felix,
however, is different. Felix was a rhetorician with an

orotund capacity, and he made his book, *Felix on the Bat*, a very gentlemanly piece of eloquence. Quotations abound in it, and the first chapter, on "Batting", begins like this:

"Miserable indeed must that age be in which the empire of the women is lost, and in which the judgment of the fairer sex is counted as nothing. . . . Glance your eye over the civilised portions of this globe, and you will be struck with the beautiful conviction that where the fairer sex are admitted to witness the happiness of those who, escaping from the turmoil of business, essay to shake off the monotonous responsibilities of their different avocations by healthful recreation, there the character of the men receives a much higher tone, and, animated with an additional spirit by their presence and by the smile of their encouraging approbation, cheerfulness pervades the sport. Long may the customs of our land suffer them to come amongst us, and long may the manliness of this noble game deserve their patronising influence!"

The gallant Felix! Yet the glory of his book is not his courteous and polished pen, but the coloured plates of gentlemen making correct strokes, beneath (no doubt) the eyes of the fascinated and enthusiastic fair—with the famous frontispiece of Felix riding high above a cricket field, Ariel-like, on a flitter-mouse—*Felix on the Bat*.[1]

I mentioned just now William Bolland's book which is valuable for containing Old Clarke's letter on bowling, and interesting both in itself and because William Bolland, Esq., was in real life Thackeray's Fred Bayham. One

[1] When living at Blackheath, where he kept a school, Wanostrocht, or Felix, befriended the youthful George Frederick Watts, afterwards the R.A. and English Old Master; and Watts made to his specification the series of drawings of batsmen in action which appear in the book. Four depict Felix himself, Fuller Pilch and Alfred Mynn being also represented. Five of the originals hang in the Pavilion at Lord's.

[E.V.L. in *English Leaves*, 1933]

story told by this gentleman is worth repeating: Eleven
Greenwich pensioners with only one leg were playing
eleven Greenwich pensioners with only one arm, and the
one-legged men won. During the match one of the
batting veterans lost his leg as he ran between the wickets,
but, like Witherington, he fought upon his stump, for he
hopped on to complete his run. Before, however, he could
do so, the one-armed point had seized the wooden limb
and thrown down the wicket with it—with an aim worthy
of Long John Silver, under somewhat dissimilar conditions,
but with the identical missile. Now comes the tragedy:
the dastard umpire gave the hero out—under what rule
neither I nor Fred Bayham have the slightest notion. It is
said that the poor man "wept aloud" as he buckled on his
leg once more. Had he sworn, surely Uncle Toby's angel
would have dropped again his obliterating tear.

So much for the printed matter of this collection, which
runs, I suppose, to thousands of volumes. Let me close my
bee-like sippings at its sweets with a few words from the
letter of Mary Turner, of East Hoadly, in Sussex, to her son
Philip at Brighton, on September 2, 1789, which I once
placed with so much pleasure on the title-page of a reprint
of Nyren. She begins thus: "According to my promises
have sent you one piece of nankeen and a few peares,
wich I hope will com safe to hand. Last Munday"—and
this is the golden heart of this old missive—"last Munday
youre Father was at Mr Payn's and plaid at cricket, and
came home pleased anuf, for he struck the best ball in the
game, and whishd he had not anny thing else to do he would
play at cricket all his life." There is the true spirit: "All
his life." I too.

I too; but of course it cannot be. Father Time sees to
that; and during the snowstorm in which I write these lines

the unlikelihood of the sun ever shining again on my flannelled limbs is peculiarly emphatic. It is a nightmare that pursues me through every autumn, winter, and early spring. How can there be another season? one asks one's self; just as years ago, a fortnight before the holidays, one was convinced that the end of the world must intervene. The difference between the child and the middle-aged man merely is that the child expects the end of the world—the man the end of himself.

Looking out of the frosted windows of memory, in these days of colds and pessimism—the cricketer's dark ages—I seem to see most clearly the gentleman visitor who came over with the B—— team in June and hit me out of the ground twice in the first over. He was the more notable because his appearance conveyed nothing of his merit. The only danger signal was the blazer of a well-known touring club; but I am old enough to know how fallacious can be the testimony of a blazer. The biggest muff in the field can wear the best colours. He walked to the wicket without any particular confidence; but I was conscious of a twinge as I saw his swift glance round the field. He then hit my first ball clean out of it; from my second he made two; from the third another two; the fourth and fifth wanted playing; and the sixth he hit over my head among some distant haymakers. Altogether he made 68.

These gentlemen strangers are the second things we always look for as the enemy's brake draws up at the gate. The first thing we look for is the fast bowler. If he is absent our hearts give a bound, and then we are free, with less trepidation, to examine the foe for surprises. Now it is that our eyes search out the strangers and size them up. Half the subsidiary fun of village cricket—counting the game itself as the primary fun—lies in noting the difference, or resemblance, between our fears as to these strangers and their performance; and it is intensified when they are gentlemen visitors. Because, in a kind of inarticulate way, we are democrats; we do not want gentlemen visitors, although they are welcome enough when they come. Hence to see the genuine half-holiday player getting the better of the gentleman visitor pleases us. Our regular gentlemen antagonists—residents whom we know and have long striven with—we welcome all the way; it is these aliens from public schools and universities, who have had the benefit of the best training and know all the tricks and slang of the game, whom we a little resent and in whose discomfiture we delight.

The contents of the visiting brake is not always a surprise. There are occasions—particularly before a return match when the first was won by ourselves—when tidings reach us over-night that our foes are (in the pleasant cricket idiom) "mixing it up hot" for us, and are going to borrow D and C from E, E having no match on the morrow. Some flushed scout brings the news into the village on his bicycle and it spreads like fire. It is then that the glance which we throw towards the brake the next day is exceptionally keen.

Now and then it happens, of course, that the gentleman visitor has a name famous in history—a county man or an Old Blue. But the ironical stars, whose interest in cricket never fails, see to it that these do not trouble us much. By a curious chance, amounting almost to a law, none of the great cracks bat so well among villagers as in the first-class game. It is partly, as I say, the work of the stars, but not a little credit must be given to our umpires. The most illustrious of batsmen at this moment was telling me last year, during an interval at Lord's, how in a village game on the previous Saturday he had been given out leg-before for stepping across his wicket to a wide-pitched ball and bending his pads down to it in the approved (but very vile) first-class manner. "How's that?" the scandalised bowler had asked, and the umpire, chosen probably for his courageous orthodoxy with regard to pad and leather, deeming every union illicit, had immediately given the only answer possible to his almost episcopal mind: "Hout."

It is probable, if the truth were known, that more county matches have been won by umpires than either batsmen or bowlers; so what must it be in our untutored variety of the game, where umpires are chosen less from fitness to adjudicate than from mere bodily presence on the field at the given moment—so rarely the time, and the place, and the just one altogether! None the less, with all their incredible stupidity and nepotism, I take immense pleasure in village umpires, and can honestly say that never have I questioned their decisions against me or shown any anger at their mistakes. I do not say this boastingly, because, after all, one must play the game; but I could wish that others were as free from that particular fault. The last thing but one that village cricketers learn is to judge a run. The last thing, is to be decent to their umpires. If I were a squire or parson with the village school under my thumb, I should compromise with the theologians by having a class in manners at which behaviour to umpires should be taught just as spelling and ciphering are taught. A boy who behaved well to an umpire would behave well to every one. Christianity would follow automatically.

One Day and Another. 1909

DICKENS AND CRICKET

ACCORDING to tradition, the sloping meadow to the south of Gad's Hill Place, where Miss Burt's pupils now pursue and belabour the hockey-ball, was in Dickens's time a cricket-ground; and the squire is said to have played there. But this, on the evidence of *Pickwick*, I doubt; or at any rate I doubt if he did more than perform the very unusual task credited to him, of bowling the first ball and then retiring, as he may be seen doing in one of the cricket pictures in Sir Jeremiah Colman's collection.

The odd things that happened when All-Muggleton met Dingley Dell convince me that the Inimitable, much as he knew of everything else, was not even a theoretical cricketer. Otherwise the Dingley Dell XI would not, as they apparently did, surrender the match without an innings, nor would every hit made by Dumkins and Podder have had such a strange sequel. My own guess is that Dickens would have left cricket out of the book altogether had not his publishers, Mr Chapman and Mr Hall, with their early leanings towards comic sport, insisted upon it. Still, since Jingle was present with his story of Sir Thomas Blazo and the tragic end of Quanko Sambo, nothing matters.

Pleasure Trove. 1935

A RHAPSODIST AT LORD'S

To the readers of the memoir of the late Francis Thompson which stands as preface to the volume of his *Selected Poems*, it must have come as a surprise to learn that this rapt celebrant of the soul was, if not himself a cricketer, a very keen student of the game. They would have felt surprise not because there is anything irreconcilable between the life spiritual and this noble pastime, but because one naturally falls into the habit of thinking of men in one direction only and Thompson's name carried with it the idea rather of midnight visions than of the sunlit pitch.

But literary genius and love of cricket have joined hands before. Cowper at Westminster was eager for the game. Byron played for Harrow against Eton. Mr Meredith, whose cricket enthusiasm flushes through his novels, was, he has told me, an alert fieldsman at the point of the bat; while Mr Barrie, it is well known, goes so far as to possess a team of his own whose merits he has described in an illustrated *brochure* which is at once the joy of those who own it and the despair of those who do not. Two instances of what I may call wholly unexpected cricketers may be added. Mr Lang, by whose cradle the muse of the game, benignantly smiling, most assuredly stood with gifts in her hand, has discovered that Cuchulainn, the Irish hero, played, and naturally excelled, at cricket in its most primitive form about 200 A.D., while (and here we come nigher the poet of *The Hound of Heaven*) if you look in Mr Philip Norman's fascinating history of the West Kent Cricket Club you will find the name and fame of one H. E. Manning, afterwards Cardinal.

None the less it was a surprise to many persons, as I say, to find that Francis Thompson was a devotee too; and to those who had seen him in the flesh (and in the ulster which he did not don until the swallows were with us nor doff until they had flown) the surprise must have been greater still, since from such an exterior it would require a reader of men of supernatural acumen to deduce a love of open-air sport. For of all men Francis Thompson was to the casual observer least like a cricketer. It was not only this inverted affection for his overcoat; it was the whole effect, the *ensemble*, as Whitman would say. If ever a figure seemed to say "Take me anywhere in the world so long as it is not to a cricket match," that was Francis Thompson's. And his eye supported it. His eye had no brightness: it swung laboriously upon its object; whereas the enthusiasts of St John's Wood dart their glances like birds.

But Francis Thompson was born to baffle the glib inference. With his heart warmed by the very presence of God he could sell matches at Charing Cross. The world, which at every turn seemed to have crushed him beneath its cold weight, he had mastered and disdained while still a youth. Fate might beat against his frame, but within blossomed the rose. He carried his consolations.

Latterly he went seldom to Lord's. His memories were sad. It was indeed from this sadness, this regret for the past and unwillingness to recall it too vividly, that was born the poem a stanza of which was printed in the *Athenaeum*, and which, with other verses on the game, I am permitted to print in full here. The poem is not dated, but it is recent. As I understand the case, Thompson had been invited to Lord's to see Middlesex and Lancashire, and had agreed to go; but as the time drew near he found he could not face the ordeal. Such a mood imports a new note into cricket poetry. Cricket poetry hitherto has been descriptive, reflective, rapturous, gay, humorous. It has never before to my knowledge been made a vehicle for a lament for the past of profoundest melancholy.

Every one knows the sadness of the backward look—every one has lost friends both of kin and of the soul. But the cricket enthusiast (and this applies to other spectacular games and sports too), whether he plays or merely watches, has had two pasts, two chances of bereavement—his own private losses, and the losses that have been suffered by the game. It is impossible for a quite ordinary enthusiast to see one match without thinking of an earlier: how much more then must a poet do so? The simplest and most prosaic of us, whose lives have been fortunate, cannot go to Lord's and regret no missing face upon the field. How have we, for example, yearned for Mr Stoddart these many seasons past! But Thompson. . . .

Francis Thompson was Lancashire born; as a boy he haunted the Old Trafford ground. Then came the realities of life, which in many cases were too much for him: his body was frail, he suffered almost constant pain, he was un- fitted doubly—physically and temperamentally—for mun- dane struggle. He left Ushaw, made a futile experiment or two to earn his living in the ordinary way, and drifted to London, where he fell upon the hardest times, always, however (in the beautiful image that Pater uses of Marius), protecting unsullied the white bird in his breast, always secure in his soul, but none the less conscious too that things were not as they should be with him and as they had promised to be in the days before thought, before the real fight, began—in the days when Hornby and Barlow went in first for Lancashire. To know all this is to find the

first and last stanzas of the poem which follows almost
unbearably sad.

It is little I repair to the matches of the Southron folk,
  Though my own red roses there may blow;
It is little I repair to the matches of the Southron folk,
  Though the red roses crest the caps, I know.
For the field is full of shades as I near the shadowy coast,
And a ghostly batsman plays to the bowling of a ghost,
And I look through my tears on a soundless-clapping host,
    As the run-stealers flicker to and fro,
        To and fro:—
    O my Hornby and my Barlow long ago!

It is Glo'ster coming North, the irresistible,
  The Shire of the Graces, long ago!
It is Gloucestershire up North, the irresistible,
  And new-risen Lancashire the foe!
A Shire so young that has scarce impressed its traces,
Ah, how shall it stand before all resistless Graces?
O, little red rose, their bats are as maces
  To beat thee down, this summer long ago!

This day of seventy-eight they are come up North against thee,
  This day of seventy-eight, long ago!
The champion of the centuries, he cometh up against thee,
  With his brethren, every one a famous foe!
The long-whiskered Doctor, that laugheth rules to scorn,
While the bowler, pitched against him, bans the day that he was born;
And G.F. with his science makes the fairest length forlorn;
  They are come from the West to work thee woe!

It is little I repair to the matches of the Southron folk,
  Though my own red roses there may blow;
It is little I repair to the matches of the Southron folk,
  Though the red roses crest the caps, I know.
For the field is full of shades as I near the shadowy coast,
And a ghostly batsman plays to the bowling of a ghost,
And I look through my tears on a soundless-clapping host,
    As the run-stealers flicker to and fro,
        To and fro:—
    O my Hornby and my Barlow long ago!

I might say that the match in question was played at
Old Trafford on July 25, 26, 27, 1878, when the poet was
eighteen. (He was born in December, 1859). It was an
historic contest, for the two counties had never before met.
The fame of the Graces was such that 16,000 people were
present on the Saturday, the third day—of whom, by the
way, 2000 did not pay but took the ground by storm. The
result was a draw, a little in Lancashire's favour, after a
very determined fight interrupted now and then by rain. It
was eminently Hornby's and Barlow's match. In the first
innings the amateur made only 5, but Barlow went right
through it, his wicket falling last for 40. In the second
innings Hornby was at his best, making with incredible
dash 100 out of 156 while he was in, Barlow supporting
him while he made 80 of them. In this match W.G. made
32 and 58 not out and took 4 wickets, and E.M. made 21
and 4 and took 4 wickets. G.F. played too, but it was not
his day.

The note-book in which the verses are written contains
many variations upon several of the lines.

> *O my Hornby and my Barlow long ago!*

becomes in one case

> *O my Monkey and Stone-waller long ago!*

"Monkey" was, of course, Mr Hornby's nickname. "First
he runs you out of breath," said the professional, possibly
Barlow himself, "first he runs you out of breath, then he
runs you out, and then he gives you a sovereign." A brave
summary! In what other verse he and Barlow have a place
I do not know, but they should be proud of this. It is something to have brought tears to the eyes of the poet of *Sister
Songs*. He, that unworldly ecstatic visionary, is no more,

but both cricketers are happily alive to-day—(I was talking to Barlow only last year, and such was his vivacity he seemed to have drunk of the fountain of youth)—and they may read these verses. I hope they will, although cricketers, in my experience, however they may have taken of late to writing of their game, read as little as they can.

The second piece is a description, in very easy couplets, of the great match between Middlesex and Yorkshire at Lord's on May 28, 1899. It was never intended for print: it was merely a versified memorandum of the match for the writer's own amusement. As will some day be seen, his note-books took count of most of his experiences, trivial as well as serious. A few lines may be quoted. Albert Trott, it will be remembered, after Warner had paved the way by making an historic 150, hit up in hurricane style 164. The rhymes thus describe his innings:

> *For Trott, who also month-long kept*
> *Inert, as the batsman in him slept,*
> *Wakes, and with tumult of his waking,*
> *The many-girded ground is shaking!*
> *With rolling claps and clamour, as soar*
> *Fours after fours, and ever four!*
> *Bowls Rhodes, bowls Jackson, Haigh bowls, Hirst,—*
> *To him the last is as the first:*
> *West-end tent or pavilion-rail,*
> *He lashes them home with a thresher's flail.*

I omit a curious interlude in which the psychological state of Lord Hawke, as captain, is delineated: not too accurately, I fancy, for his lordship, if I know anything about him, can meet adversity with philosophic calm. This is the end:

> *Trott keeps them trotting, till his d——d score*
> *Is just one hundred, sixty, and four,—*

The highest tally this match has scored,
And the century fourth is long up on the board.
Thank Heaven, the fellow's grown reckless now,
Jumps and slogs at them anyhow:
Two narrow shaves, amid frenzied howl
Of jubilant people, and lordly growl;
Till a clinker tingles in Brown's left hand—
Good Brown! you have snapped the infernal stand!
The last two wickets go tedious down,
And my lord strides off with his teeth and frown.

The poet throughout, although no Southerner, is against
Yorkshire; the old championship of the Red Rose against
the White coming out very strongly. The match ended
in a victory for Middlesex by an innings and 2 runs. It
was Trott's game, for not only did he score his 164 (137
of them in an hour and a half), but he took altogether nine
wickets.

The third piece is a *tour de force*, an imitation of Fitzgerald's *Omar*. Thompson, who was not given to filling
other men's moulds, began it evidently as a joke, for he
gave it a comic title, "Rime o' bat of O my sky-em". But
his mind was too powerful and proud for imitation or
sustained *facetiae*, and he quickly became individual and
human, so that the stanzas, although a parody in form,
are also a new and independent thing. They seem to me to
have no little charm. Cricket no doubt has been moralised
before—indeed is there not Fred Lillywhite's epitaph in
Highgate Cemetery?—but never so sweetly and reasonably.

PART I

Wake! for the Ruddy Ball has taken flight
That scatters the slow Wicket of the Night;
*   And the swift Batsman of the Dawn has driven*
Against the Star-spiked Rails a fiery Smite.

Wake, my Beloved! take the Bat that clears
The sluggish Liver, and Dyspeptics cheers:
    To-morrow? Why, to-morrow I may be
Myself with Hambledon and all its Peers.

To-day a Score of Batsmen brings, you say?
Yes, but where leaves the Bats of yesterday?
    And this same summer day that brings a Knight
May take the Grace and Ranjitsinjh away.

Willsher the famed is gone with all his "throws."
And Alfred's Six-foot Reach where no man knows;
    And Hornby—that great hitter—his own Son
Plays in his place, yet recks not the Red Rose.

And Silver Billy, Fuller Pilch and Small,
Alike the pigmy Briggs and Ulyett tall,
    Have swung their Bats an hour or two before,
But none played out the last and silent Ball.

Well, let them Perish! What have we to do
With Gilbert Grace the Great, or that Hindu?
    Let Hirst and Spooner slog them as they list,
Or Warren bowl his "snorter"; care not you!

With me along the Strip of Herbage strown,
That is not laid or watered, rolled or sown,
    Where name of Lord's and Oval is forgot,
And peace to Nicholas on his bomb-girt Throne.

A level Wicket, as the Ground allow,
A driving Bat, a lively Ball, and thou
    Before me bowling on the Cricket-pitch—
O Cricket-pitch were Paradise enow!

PART II

I listened where the Grass was shaven small,
And heard the Bat that groaned against the Ball:
    Thou pitchest Here and There, and Left and Right,
Nor deem I where the Spot thou next may'st Fall.

I

Forward I play, and Back, and Left and Right,
And overthrown at once, or stay till Night:
But this I know, where nothing else I know,
The last is Thine, how so the Bat shall smite.

This thing is sure, where nothing else is sure,
The boldest Bat may but a Space endure;
And he who One or who a Hundred hits
Falleth at ending to thy Force or Lure.

Wherefore am I allotted but a Day
To taste Delight, and make so brief a stay;
For meed of all my labour laid aside,
Ended alike the Player and the Play.

Behold, there is an Arm behind the Ball,
Nor the Bat's Stroke of its own Striking all;
And who the Gamesters, to what end the Game,
I think thereof our witting is but small.

Against the Attack and Twist of Circumstance
Though I oppose Defence and Shifty Glance,
What Power gives Nerve to me, and what Assaults,—
This is the Riddle. Let dull bats cry "Chance."

Is there a Foe that (domineers) the Ball?
And one that Shapes and wields us Willows all?
Be patient if Thy Creature in Thy Hand
Break, and the so-long-guarded Wicket fall!

Thus spoke the Bat. Perchance a foolish Speech
And wooden, for a Bat has straitened Reach:
Yet thought I, I had heard Philosophers
Prate much on this wise, and aspire to Teach.

Ah, let us take our Stand, and play the Game,
But rather for the Cause than for the Fame;
Albeit right evil is the Ground, and we
Know our Defence thereon will be but lame.

O Love, if thou and I could but Conspire
Against this Pitch of Life, so false with Mire,
Would we not Doctor it afresh, and then
Roll it out smoother to the Bat's Desire?

I suppose that the Knight whom Thompson had in mind was Albert Knight of Leicestershire, whose writings on cricket he greatly admired. Willsher was Edgar Willsher, "The Lion of Kent", and a member of the All England team, born in 1828. A "fast and ripping" left-handed round-arm bowler, in or about 1857, his style came under severe criticism in *Bell's Life*, but he survived the attack. Mr Haygarth calls him "one of the most amiable, as well as one of the staunchest, of cricketers in the world".

To the name of Alfred the poet himself has put the following glowing footnote:

"Alfred is Alfred the Great, Alfred Mynn, W.G. of his day; six foot two, shoulder of mutton fist, foot on which he leaned made a grave in soft turf, brilliant both as bat and fast bowler."

The younger Hornby—A.H.—is captain of Lancashire. Silver Billy was William Beldham, of the Hambledon Club, over whose genius Nyren becomes lyrical. He lived to a very great age and died in 1860. Fuller Pilch, a Norfolk man by birth, was the best bat in England between 1820 and 1850. He played for Kent in the thirties and forties, and died at Canterbury in 1870:

> *Land of Hops, you hold in trust*
> *Very sacred human dust!*

There were two Smalls, both Hambledon men, celebrated by Nyren. Briggs was of course Johnny Briggs, of Thompson's own county, the left-handed bowler and cover-point whose end was a tragedy, for he lost his reason through a sunstroke and died in an asylum. George Ulyett is dead too—the great and genial Yorkshireman of the seventies. The other names need no gloss.

Those are the verses. Thompson wrote also a little prose on the game, including a lengthy criticism of the *Jubilee Book of Cricket*. This review, printed in the *Academy*, for September 4, 1897, is interesting not only on the literary side but for its theoretical acumen too. It contains a very minute examination of the differences between the pitched-up balls of the under-arm and the over-arm bowler, and there are some discerning remarks upon back and forward play. But more to our purpose as illustrating Thompson's cricket prose is the passage in praise of Vernon Royle, another Lancashire man, at cover-point:

Fine fielding is very largely the work of a captain who is himself a fine fielder, and knows its vast importance in winning matches. Many a match has been won rather in the field than at the wicket. And, if only a boy will set himself really to study its niceties, it is a most fascinating branch of cricket. Prince Ranjitsinhji remarks on the splendid opportunities of cover-point, and cites the Rev. Vernon Royle as the cover-point to whom all cricketers give the palm during the last thirty years. "From what one hears," he says, "he must have been a magnificent fielder." He was. And I notice the fact, because Vernon Royle may be regarded as a concrete example of the typical fielder, and the typical fielder's value. He was a pretty and stylish bat; but it was for his wonderful fielding that he was played. A ball for which hardly another cover-point would think of trying, he flashed upon, and with a single action stopped it and returned it to the wicket. So placed that only a single stump was visible to him, he would throw that down with unfailing accuracy, and without the slightest pause for aim. One of the members of the Australian team in Royle's era, playing against Lancashire, shaped to start for a hit wide of cover-point. "No, no!" cried his partner; "the policeman is there!" There were no short runs

anywhere in the neighbourhood of Royle. He simply
terrorised the batsmen; nor was there any necessity for an
extra cover—now so constantly employed. In addition
to his sureness and swiftness, his style was a miracle of
grace. Slender and symmetrical, he moved with the light-
ness of a young roe, the flexuous elegance of a leopard—
it was a sight for an artist or a poet to see him field. Briggs,
at his best, fell not far short in efficiency; but there was no
comparison between the two in style and elegance. To be a
fielder like Vernon Royle is as much worth any youth's
endeavours as to be a batsman like Ranjitsinhji, or a bowler
like Richardson.

That the author of *The Hound of Heaven* and *The Anthem
of Earth* should be also the most ingenious and suggestive
reviewer of Prince Ranjitsinhji's work is a curious circumstance worthy of note by any Isaac Disraeli of the future,
who should also make a memorandum of the circumstance
that when this rapturous visionary lay dying in the Roman
Catholic hospital in St John's Wood the volume which he
asked for and kept within touch beneath his pillow was Mr
Jacobs's *Many Cargoes*.

One Day and Another. 1909

THE INDIAN NYREN

MOHUMMUD ABDULLAH KHAN'S Cricket Guide was published in Lucknow in 1891, the full title being *Cricket Guide intended for the use of Young Players, containing a Short but Comprehensive Account of the Game, embracing all the important Rules and Directions nicely arranged in due Succession.* The reason given by the Indian Nyren for putting forth this work was the wish to allay the fever which cricket seems then to have been provoking in his compatriots. Those who remember the *sang-froid*, the composed mastery, of Prince Ranjitsinhji may be surprised to learn that, at any rate in 1891, cricket had a way of rushing to young India's head. "Even those," wrote Mohummud Abdullah Khan, "who are very good and noble (say, next-door to angels) turn so rash and inconsiderate at certain moments that their brains lose the balance and begin to take fallacious fancies." More, they "boil over with rage, pick up quarrels with one another, and even look daggers at their own dearest friends and darlings," the cause being not only the game itself, but an ignorance of the laws that should govern it and them, and without obedience to which "a human body is nothing but a solid piece of rocky hill, that is to say 'cleverness'." Very well, then. Feeling as he did about it, Mohummud Abdullah Khan had no alternative but to write his book.

Practical as the instructions of this Oriental teacher can be, it is deportment that really lies nearest his heart. He is as severe on a want of seriousness as upon loss of temper. Thus, he says: "The fielders must take especial care not to exchange jokes with one another or try funny tricks that do

secretly divide their attention and produce a horrible defect
in their fielding." Again, "Behave like gentlemen after the
game is over; avoid clapping and laughing in faces of the
persons you have defeated." But there is no harm in a
match being momentarily interrupted by a touch of courtesy. Thus: "If you are the Captain of your team and the
fielders of the opposite party clap your welcome, you are
required simply to turn or raise your night cap a little, and
this is sufficient to prove your easy turn of disposition as
well as to furnish the return of their compliments."

For the most part the directions are sound, even if they
may be a little obscure in statement; but now and then one
is puzzled. The game in India must have been animated
indeed if no error has crept into the following note on the
bowler: "During one and the same over the bowler is
allowed to change his ends as often as he may desire, but
cannot possibly bowl two overs in succession." And this
reads oddly: "The bowler is allowed to make the batsman
stand in any direction he may choose from the wicket he is
bowling from." But no fault can be found here: "The
bowler must always try to pitch his ball in such style and
position that its spring may always rest on the wickets to
be aimed at. He must know the proper rules of *no balls* and
wides and"—here we are again!—"must never be wishing
to pick up any quarrel with the umpire of the opposite
party."

And so we reach the umpires, upon whom the author
becomes very earnest. Under the frenetic conditions to
which cricket could reduce his countrymen, to act as umpire was no joke. Indeed he goes so far as to advise the
reader never to fill that position except when the match is
between teams personally unknown to him. For to umpire
among friends is to turn those friends to foes. "Take special

care, my dear umpires, not to call *over* unless the ball has finally settled in the wicket-keeper's hand, as well as avoid ordering a batsman *out* unless you are appealed to by the opposite party. . . . Each and every one of the umpires must avoid using insulting terms, or playing on bets with any one of the fielders or persons in general, in his capacity of being an umpire."

The requirements of a perfect wicket-keeper are well set forth. After describing his somewhat "stooping condition" the mentor says, "I would like this man to be of a grave demeanour and humble mind, say the Captain of the Club, whose duties are to guide the fielders, order the change of their places if necessary," and "guard himself well against the furious attacks of the sweeping balls." Here Mohummud Abdullah Khan is among some of the best critics, who have always held that for the captain to be wicket-keeper (as, for example, in the case of Gregor MacGregor) is an ideal arrangement.

Point also needs some special qualities: "He must be a very smart and very clever man, of a quick sight and slender form." (Slender form? And yet one has seen W.G. doing not so badly there!) "His place is in front of the popping-crease, about seven yards from the striker. He must take special care to protect his own person in case when fast bowling is raging through the field. Pay great attention to the game, my dear pointer, or suppose yourself already hurt."

Giving and Receiving. 1922

REMINISCENCES

(i) PYCROFT

THE very first author of a book—and as it happened a book I possessed and knew by heart—that I ever saw was the Rev. James Pycroft, who wrote *The Cricket-Field*. And it was in the cricket field that I used to see him, when I was a small boy of eight and he was a man of sixty-three: the County Ground at Hove. He was erect and active, with a pink face and the whitest hair and whiskers, a clergyman's black cape and tall hat. His habit was to walk round the ground, with frequent pauses as the ball was being delivered, usually alone but often talking animatedly with some old crony from the pavilion, where he was apparently too restless to sit. Many, many years later, when compiling an enthusiastic record of early cricket called *The Hambledon Men*, I was to find *The Cricket-Field* of great service.

Reading, Writing and Remembering. 1932

(ii) ANDREW LANG

Later I came to know Lang personally: not well, but well enough to receive a number of unsolicited letters from him and one day to go with him to Lord's. We sat on one of the front benches of the Pavilion. He wore an ancient top hat, which he tilted over his eyes, stretched his legs on the seat in front and talked all the while; but I had no notion of what he was saying, partly because of his careless utterance and partly because I was watching the game. Cricket demands concentration. He had a voice that did not carry—"roupy" he himself called it—and he did something to his words too: bit them, I think, so that most of them were lost.

Reading, Writing and Remembering. 1932

(iii) CONRAD

I did not see him again until not long before he died and under very unexpected conditions, for it was in the Kent county cricket ground during the Canterbury week.

For the most part this ground is a mass-meeting of motor-cars, but on this afternoon the placidity of the game was suddenly broken into by the notes of a guard's horn, and in rolled a coach-and-four driven by a benign gentleman in gold spectacles and a white hat who might almost have come over from Dingley Dell. Behind him, on the next seat, was a distinguished bearded foreigner, amusedly surveying the scene through a single eyeglass. When I came to look again I saw that the driver was J. B. Pinker, the literary agent, and the distinguished bearded foreigner was Joseph Conrad. After the horses had been taken out and the vehicle was transformed into a private box, I joined the party, and for an hour or so sat with Conrad and did my best to qualify him to go in first for Poland. Cricket was strange to him, but he liked the crowd, and all our excitement about such trifles as bats and balls fed his sense of irony. Again the thought struck me that there can be no defence like elaborate courtesy.

Reading, Writing and Remembering. 1932

(iv) BARRIE AND OTHERS

In *The Greenwood Hat* Barrie tells the story of his cricket team, the Allahakbarries—meaning "God help us"—of which I was a member. We used to play the artists and various elevens brought together for the purpose. We played at Shere, at Esher, at Frensham Ponds, at Farnham, at Shackleford—all in Surrey—and were not distressed by defeat. J. C. Snaith, who had been tried for Notts, was our trump card with the ball, but Barrie bowled slow left, with an action very like J. C. White of Somerset and England, and had to be watched. Will Meredith, George Meredith's son, kept wicket with a magnificent composure and disdain of byes; C. T. Smith (who under the name of Charles Turley writes some of the best school stories) wherever he stood fielded like a county player; Conan Doyle, who was very good, was our best all-rounder, and Harry Graham, the librettist, batted as though he had been properly taught. Another useful man was Walter Frith, son of the painter of "Derby Day". Barrie's little privately printed book describing the members of the original team, of which I was not one, and their first antagonists, an eleven brought together by Mary Anderson at Broadway, is now very rare and a collector's piece, fetching three figures. In addition to regular players, there were occasional extra men, such as Charles Whibley, who was said by his captain, adapting a well-known phrase, to hit "blooming hard, blooming high and blooming seldom", and Hewlett, who used to turn out in perfect flannels but was not proficient.

Among the artists, who, since they never do anything to tire them, were always stronger than their adversaries, the chief scores were made by Henry Ford, the illustrator of Andrew Lang's fairy books. They also had, in G. H. Swinstead, a formidable performer with both bat and ball. H. H. La Thangue was one of their keenest supporters. E. A. Abbey was usually captain, bringing into the game all his American energy and a terrifying velocity in throwing which he had acquired at baseball; but otherwise he was not to be feared.

Reading, Writing and Remembering.　1932

IMAGINATION AND FANCY

AN OLD CRICKETER TALKS

"Who would you call the best bowler of your time?" I asked.

"Take him all round," he said, "Alfred Shaw. He never tired and he never lost his length. And the ball used to come off the pitch much quicker than you were expecting, with a terrible lot of work still on it. He could drop it on a shilling twelve times out of twelve; gentlemen used to lay one down for him. He was wise too; you can't help being wise with a long nose like that; he watched the game like a captain. Late in his life he was taken up by Lord Sheffield, the one who was so keen about cricket, who fetched him to Sussex to coach for the Club and ended by making a friend of him. Couldn't do anything without Alfred Shaw. I remember Shaw telling me about how they went to the North Pole in his Lordship's yacht and played cricket there by the light of the midnight sun."

"Using the Pole as a wicket, I suppose," I suggested.

"Yes," he said. "Shaw told me about it. He played a bit for Sussex in those days, but what he did as a bowler he lost in the field. Couldn't get down to them. It's a mistake to go on too long, but it's a very sad day when one has to retire. One's at the same time too old and too young. Too old for games but too young and inexperienced and too fond of the excitement and applause to settle down to a new life. That's why—well, that accounts for some of the mishaps. I was lucky; I was able to succeed my father here."

"Was he a cricketer too?" I asked.

"Yes," he said. "In his day. Round-arm. He had played

143

with Alfred Mynn and the old Nonpareil. He called us throwers.

"Talking about Shaw reminds me that I used to like the Trent Bridge match the best of all our out-matches," he resumed, "because of the glee parties. The Notts professionals in my day were crazy about singing and they used to meet at Mordecai Sherwin's public-house and sing and sing like good 'uns. I don't suppose cricketers do that kind of thing now, except perhaps on the steamers when they go abroad. There wasn't any Bridge in my time, although we played Nap on railway journeys. Gunn was a great singer; so was Arthur Shrewsbury.

"Sherwin kept wicket, you remember, but the great day of his life, he used to tell us, was when he was put on to bowl at Lord's in the Middlesex and Notts match in 1892 to try and break up a terrible long stand between Mr Webbe and Mr Stoddart. I had the luck to be there. I ought to have been playing for my own county, but I was called as a witness in a case at the Law Courts. I remember how mad I was about it at the time, but how glad I was afterwards to have been able to get to Lord's in the late afternoon.

"It was a wonderful match, the way it went. Notts had made 466, of which Arthur Shrewsbury got 212 and Mr Robinson 72. Then Middlesex went in, and as they only made 195 they had to follow on.

"It was just after their second innings began that I got to the ground, and things were going pretty well. Mr T. C. O'Brien—as he was then, he became Sir Timothy later—was bringing off some of his own special late cuts and Mr Stoddart was putting the thick of his bat behind the straight ones and driving them to long on and long off as only he could do. His back play could be wonderful!

I remember one ball he had to play back to, hitting the Pavilion railings and rebounding forty yards. There's strength for you! Well, Mr O'Brien left when he had made 57, but even then no one thought it could be anything but a drawn game. The score was 152 for five when Mr Webbe came in and, as we say now, dug himself in, so that with only half an hour's play left, Mr Stoddart and he had added nearly another hundred, and Middlesex looked as safe as a bank.

"Then one of those surprising things happened which you have to go to a cricket match to see. The score was 244 for five when Mr Robinson, the Notts captain, gave Mordecai the chance of his life. 'Take off your pads,' he said, 'and see what you can do with the ball, and I'll keep wicket.'

"Mordecai being only a stumper, none of the Middlesex crowd expected any trouble; so you can think what a shock they had when in his first over he clean bowled Mr Webbe! Mr Webbe had been defying Attewell and Shacklock for an hour, for 32, and the wicket-keeper got him! That's cricket all over. The ball looked simple enough, but it got off the pitch very sharp. Sheer luck!

"The crowd took it like one between the eyes. They were stunned. Nothing could be heard but a few stray Nottingham yells.

"Rawlin now came in. Imagine what the crowd felt when in the next over Attewell, who had been bowling all day like a book, without any luck, got Mr Stoddart leg before. Seven for 247. People began to look at their watches then, I can tell you. You could see in the hush every hand going to the waistcoat pocket for that purpose. Those were the days before wars and wrist-watches, you must remember.

K

"Three men to come in and ten minutes to go—ten minutes for Notts to get them out, ten minutes for the Middlesex tail to keep its end up. I was glad I wasn't one of the hairs of that tail.

"Mr Thesiger—he's Lord Chelmsford now—took Mr Stoddart's place and got a single off Attewell, which took him to the other end opposite Mordecai, and in the next over he watched him as though he was Spofforth and Lohmann rolled into one. Perhaps he took him too seriously and had better have had a whack, for after making two he was clean bowled.

"Then the few Nottinghamshire spectators turned Lord's into Trent Bridge, they yelled so, and the Londoners took out their watches again and never put them back. Eight for 250. Seven minutes to go and two wickets to fall.

"In came J. T. Hearne looking serious and dogged and as though this wasn't his job at all: his job was bowling. Meanwhile Rawlin was defending his wicket with the most laborious care, but with five and a half minutes to go Attewell bowled him. Nine for 252. In came Mr R. S. Lucas, who usually went in earlier, but West and Phillips, the ordinary last men, had begun the follow-on innings.

"Everything now depended on Jack Hearne and Mr Lucas, who got a four off Sherwin right away. We couldn't breathe. It ought to have been a three or a one, to get him to Jack's end; but it was a four, and in the next over Attewell put down one a little on the off, Jack slashed at it and the whole eleven called 'How's that?' It looked as though they had called too soon, for Mr Robinson fumbled it. But before it could reach the ground he got it and the game was over!

"And so this most exciting match was lost and won by

an innings, fourteen runs and four minutes, and I hope
Mr Robinson kept the ball as a souvenir; for it was more
his match than anyone's, in spite of the Shrewsbury and
Stoddart big scores.

"I went into the players' box to shake Sherwin's hand
and it was then they told me what Mr Webbe had said when
he got back to the Pavilion. 'I feel,' he said, 'as if I'd been
run over by a donkey-cart.' Sherwin never forgot that.
I've heard him tell the story of the match again and again,
but the thing he was proud of was not his bowling success
but Mr Webbe's remark. 'I feel as if I'd been run over by a
donkey-cart,' he said. 'That's rich! Those were the days,'
he sighed.

"But when I think of that great match it is not only Mr
Webbe's joke that I remember, but the tragic end of the
two greatest batsmen: Mr Stoddart and Arthur Shrewsbury. It's odd how cricketers are often not very happy
men. I suppose it's got something to do with the dis-
appointments of the game—it's glorious uncertainty, as
they call it. Uncertainty can be very depressing as well
as glorious and it makes men moody.

"So terribly chancy: a hundred one innings and out
first ball the next. And the things that happen wrong that
aren't your own fault, such as having catches dropped off
your bowling and being run out by the man you're in
with. You've got to be a philosopher, I can tell you, to
keep sweet. Wrong decisions by umpires have something
to do with it too, and then the miserable hours spent
waiting for the rain to stop or the wickets to dry."

Down the Sky. 1936

THE PAVILION CAT

THERE is at Lord's, as everyone knows, a cat. It is called the Pavilion cat. On a fine day, when the match is not important enough to crowd the ring—when, for instance, the M.C.C. are playing Glamorganshire or the Gentlemen of Scotland—the Pavilion cat has the pleasant habit of sunning itself on the turf within the ropes. At more momentous matches, such as England and Australia, or Oxford and Cambridge, or Gentlemen and Players, it pays only occasional visits to the enclosed ground, preferring the seclusion of the Pavilion. But whether visible or not, the cat is as keen an observer and follower of the game as, say, Mr Andrew Lang himself, who, by the way, once mentioned it in a poem, an adaptation of Emerson. On these days, when the cat retires to an isolated position of espionage, the sparrows which skim over the grass inside the ring and now and then flutter three feet into the air and then tumble to earth again, feel increased confidence in their amusement.

One morning the remarkable tidings came that the Pavilion cat, whom I have long admired mutely, and occasionally caressed, had suddenly become articulate. It no longer merely purred; it spoke. Hardly believing the news, I hurried to Lord's to make certain. I found the cat on the turf at the nursery end. There were feathers near it, and once or twice it licked its whiskers with gusto. Beyond doubt it had been hunting. Remembering a police-court case reported in the papers the preceding week, I opened by asking for an opinion on the question, Is a cat entitled to its first bird as a dog is to its first bite?

"Certainly," said the Pavilion cat, "but I was not in the
148

least surprised to hear that the decision went against our race. Dogs always score."

"But this," I said, "was a pigeon, not a sparrow, mind."

The cat smiled to itself—a glutinous smile—and placing its right paw on its chest, rubbed it gently. I had awakened a tender reminiscence. Once, it was clear, the Pavilion cat had partaken of pigeon, and hoped to do so again.

"A pigeon," it said at length, "alters the case a little. Only the best cats are entitled to pigeon. And canaries—I am not sure I would allow every cat a canary. You've no idea," it added, more briskly, "how much skill is needed to get a canary out of a cage. It is an art in itself. Cages are made so badly. But sparrows, yes. Every cat should be permitted one sparrow by way of a fair start. Blood is necessary."

"Necessary?" I echoed.

"Most necessary," replied the cat. "Milk is so civilising. I like that old idea of a free beginning. I am sorry they have dropped the plan of giving the first batsman in a match a trial ball."

That brought us to cricket, and I felt more at home at once. I am not casuist enough for a cat.

"What do you think of all this big scoring?" I asked; it had been a season of centuries.

"I don't like it," the cat replied. "I much prefer several double-figures to one hundred and a lot of tiny innings. Two '50's' in a score look far better than a '100' and a '0'. But there must be a tail. I insist on the tail. And that reminds me of a rather neat thing I said the other day. It was just after the Australians were all out for 18,[1] when I

[1] The Pavilion cat was referring to that lamentable June afternoon in 1896, when the Australians, playing the M.C.C., put together only 18 runs: five wickets falling to Pougher for no runs at all. Such cruel fortune was nothing short of distressing. The keenest English partisan looking on could not but regret our success. [E.V.L.]

met a Persian acquaintance of mine in the Abbey Road. She has a very small body and a tremendous brush, and I said: 'Why are you like the Australian team?' She gave it up, of course—cats always do. 'Because you are mostly tail,' I said. Wasn't that good? But she didn't seem to care for it very much: those Persians are so vain. As Mr Lyttelton said in the Pavilion the other day, 'Persicos odi'."

I hastened to turn the subject, for a cat quoting Horace is something too uncanny.

"Who is your favourite batsman?" I asked.

"Ranji," said the cat, promptly.

"Good," I replied. "Ranji is my choice too. Isn't he gorgeous?"

"Steady!" said the Pavilion cat, with some acerbity. "He's certainly very fine, but I notice a tendency to compliment him too highly. The other day, for instance, I heard a man in the ring say to another, 'Isn't Ranji a beautiful creature—as active and graceful as a cat!' Now, sir, with all due respect to Ranji, that won't do. He isn't as good as that, you know. He's very good, but he isn't as good as that."

"Of course," I said, cordially. "And who is your favourite bowler?" I added quickly, for the cat was beginning to show signs of roving attention. There were some sparrows—young ones—rather near us, and the tail of her eye was on them.

"Oh, Jack, of course. Our Jack," she said.

"Jack?" I repeated.

"Yes. J. T. Hearne. We all call him Jack here—we who know him. But why don't they put him in earlier? He's always not out. But I must be off now. I have a little business to transact over there," and it nodded in the direction of the birds.

"Another 'trial'?" I suggested. And then remembering the miracle, I added hastily, "There's one thing I want to ask you before you go, and that is, How did you come to have this gift of speech?"

"Oh, that was quite simple," said the cat; "I've been sipping some of the Broad Halfpenny punch."

"The Broad Halfpenny punch?"

"Yes; haven't you read Nyren?" the cat replied. "Don't you recollect where he says of the Broad Halfpenny punch that it could 'make a cat speak'?"

"Yes," I said, "I remember it; a magnificent passage."

"Well," continued the cat, "I've been drinking some. An old fellow brought a basket to the match yesterday—an old-fashioned Hampshire yeoman—and he scratched my head—just behind the ears, where it's so soothing—and gave me a slice of beef and a sip at his bottle. We had a most interesting conversation after that."

"By jingo!" I said. "It's the most extraordinary thing I ever heard. It makes you unique."

The cat blushed. Only those who have seen a cat blush can have any notion of what true modesty is. I then thanked it profusely and withdrew.

"By the way," it called after me, "I hope the muzzling order is not likely to go out of force just yet."

"No, I fear not," I said. "Good-bye." I felt afterwards that it was a little ungallant to say "fear", but then, you see, I have a dog.

Willow and Leather. 1898

THE WAGER

SOME of the happiest hours of Rudd's early life were spent in the Oldshire County Ground at Caston.

Mr Sergison was a great follower of cricket and he often took Rudd into the Pavilion with him, where they sat among the Oldshire patrons and came very near indeed to the great men of the world—such as Lord Harris and Jack Shuter, W. W. Read and the Hon. Ivo Bligh, the Australian giant, Bonnor, with his fair beard, and—another!

Rudd was never bored, although too young to understand the *finesse* of the game. Not even Scotton or Louis Hall could bore him. It was enough that they were batting on a green field and eleven men were trying to get them out.

Those were the days when you could pick out the professionals and the amateurs by their clothes; and an over had only four balls in it; and no cricketer dreamed of stopping to drink tea; and even W.G. could leave the pavilion without being photographed; and point stood at point; and there were often as many as four men on the on side; and no professional advertised tonics, because no professional ever took them. None the less, Rudd and the other spectators thought the game as good as it could be.

It was the custom at the Oldshire County Cricket ground —and still is, but under safer conditions—for the amateurs to have a few minutes' practice before the match began, when their ambition seemed to be not so much to defend their wickets against good bowling as to hit indifferent bowling into the empyrean. To hit high and far and often was the thing.

Any boy on the ground who chanced to possess a ball was allowed to bowl, and naturally the most famous batsmen had the greatest number of servitors.

In those days the nets extended only for a yard or so beyond the batsmen, and not, as now, for the length of the pitch, so that as there was a row of half a dozen batsmen at least, all hitting as hard as they possibly could, the position of bowler was fraught with dangers comparable to those of war. Balls whizzed in every direction at about a mile a minute, and many were the accidents. Rudd knew one boy who had lost an eye there.

One morning Rudd was early on the ground, as he liked to be, to await the Gloucestershire men; and on this day he had to be earlier still in order to secure a position at the nets with his ball, because in those brave days Gloucestershire meant W.G. True that other fine players were in the eleven, not the least of them W.G.'s elder brother, the active and resourceful E.M., so dangerous in the field, and the slender and accomplished G.F., and their cousin W. R. Gilbert; but it was W.G. who drew the crowd. His towering bulk and black beard were the loadstone, and Rudd's mind this morning was filled with the determination (weak and infirm as was his youthful arm) to make one of the Doctor's bowlers—just to be able to say he had done so.

So many bowlers were there that the great man had no time to do more than recover his footing before the next ball came along. This haste and absence of his usual careful preliminaries probably were as much the cause of the terrific thing that happened as any transcendent merit in Rudd's bowling; but be that as it may, Rudd sent down a ball, W.G. stepped out to hit, missed it, and was bowled middle stump.

Rudd glowed all day and might have been seen mys-

teriously smiling to himself no matter where he was. The
fact did not pass into his anecdotal repertory, but the
memory of the triumph was magnificently framed and hung
on the line in the gallery of his heart.

That, however, was not of the first importance, nor was
W.G. for all his glory Rudd's prime hero. His prime hero
and the first man to lift the boy to the stature and condition of a man—and a sporting man at that—was another.
But you shall hear.

It was when Rudd was ten that a match between the
Gentlemen and the Players was played at Caston for the
benefit of a great bowler who had just retired, and Rudd
was there all three days. It was one of the most remarkable contests on record, because both sides made the same
score in the first innings, and the finish was extraordinarily
close.

Rudd had seen many matches with exciting moments,
but nothing like this, nor in after life did he, much as he
frequented Lord's and the Oval, ever see another quite so
dramatic.

But it was not merely the excitement that endowed the
third day with its red letter, but the distinction which Rudd
enjoyed of sitting in the closest intimacy with his ideal
cricketer, and being treated not only as an equal but as a
gentleman and a gambler.

And who was Rudd's hero?

Rudd's hero was a shortish, very active man, with a
tanned cheek, and a small thick moustache, and very white
teeth, and a brilliant eye. He usually went in first, with
Barlow (a racehorse with a teamster), and he hit very
hard, called his partner loudly, ran very short runs, and
under no circumstances wore anything on his head.

His name?

His name was A. N. Hornby, and he was captain of Lancashire, and on this occasion captain of the Gentlemen.

Rudd saw most of the counties, but none contained a personality so fascinating to him as this impulsive Lancastrian, the ideal amateur.

The Players batted first, sending in the genial Yorkshire colossus, George Ulyett, and the cautious, polished Shrewsbury. But George fell instantly to a wily one from the insidious Mr Appleby. Then came Barnes of Notts, jovial and reckless, who rattled up thirty-six; and the plodding Selby, who was caught at the wicket by Mr Tylecote; and then Mr Hornby's patient associate Barlow, who never got out at all, partly because Mr Hornby was not with him to run him out, and partly because he took no risks, but made fifty-four in his stone-walling way; and then that winning mirthful Yorkshireman, Willy Bates, who made a light-hearted fifty; and then the greatest character of them all at that day and for long after, Tom Emmett himself, with his huge comic nose, only one remove from Carnival night, and his shambling gait, and a smile as broad as one of his own Ridings.

The last four were Charlwood of Sussex, A. Payne, the wicket-keeper, Alfred Shaw, the Ulysses of bowlers, and his dangerous fast ally, F. Morley; and the whole side made 204, Mr Appleby accounting for six of them.

The Gentlemen as a whole were less illustrious, but A. G. Steel was among them, and A. H. Trevor and G. F. Vernon (Trevor's companion in the famous Rickling Green partnership), and especially Mr Hornby, who made top score with sixty-nine, the whole side being out also for 204.

The Pavilion having buzzed for twenty minutes with the coincidence, the Players went in again. This time Mr Steel succeeded in getting Barlow caught; Ulyett made fourteen; and the chief scorers were Selby with forty-six and Bates with twenty-three. The total was a poor 112; and Mr Steel claimed seven wickets.

The weather was fair, the pitch was good, and 112 seemed a trifling total for a team of high-stepping amateurs to exceed, when the Gentlemen went to the wicket again. But the bowling and fielding turned out to be too good. Alfred Shaw, who had done nothing in the first innings, now began to be difficult; and when Mr Steel and Mr Hornby were both out for only thirty-seven between them, and the score was still low, and no remarkable batsmen were left to go in, the situation began to look serious for the amateurs.

Mr Hornby, on retiring to the Pavilion, hastily removed his pads and came out to the top row to watch. It was packed; not a seat; so, seizing Rudd, he lifted him up, insinuated himself beneath him, and placed him on his knee. Rudd flushed with pride.

"Now," Mr Hornby said, "who's going to win?"

"The Gentlemen," said Rudd loyally.

"I'm afraid not," said the prince of men. "But let's have a little bet about it, you and I. I'll bet you a penny the Players win. Are you on?"

Rudd said he was, and they settled down to witness the last desperate minutes of the struggle.

Mr Tylecote all too soon placed his leg before a straight one from Shaw, and had to go back. Mr M. P. Lucas, after making ten and raising hopes, was caught at the wicket off the same astute bowler.

The score was now 107 for nine wickets. Only six runs needed for victory; but who was to make them? The partisans of the Gentlemen trembled with fear, for the last

man was the placid Mr Appleby, whose batting powers
were only rudimentary, yet surely he was good either for
six runs himself or to stay there while Mr Bettesworth got
them! But Shaw was bowling like the devil, and there was
another ball to the over, too!

The partisans of the Players were flushed and restless.
Surely Mr Appleby could not withstand Shaw's cunning?
The very next ball might settle it all.

Meanwhile Mr Appleby allowed none of the anguish
of the moment to accelerate his movements or disturb
his serenity, but walked to the wicket with unconcern,
and took his middle.

Mr Hornby groaned. "Keep in, keep in!" he murmured
to his last man, who, being three hundred yards away,
took no notice. In a tense silence Shaw delivered the last
ball of the over, which Mr Appleby succeeded in snicking
for one.

A shout went up. Four to tie, five to win!

Mr Appleby now had to face Bates, and again Mr
Hornby groaned. "He can't bat," he said, "he can't bat.
You've lost your penny."

The fieldsmen seemed to be a week changing their
places; but at last Mr Appleby had secured his middle, and
Bates began to run. Not a sound in the place! No one even
breathed. The ball was delivered; Mr Appleby played at it
and missed it, and it missed the stumps by the varnish, as
they say. The wicket-keeper, Payne, flung up his hands to
mark the miracle. Bates took the ball again and again
bowled, and this time Mr Appleby got it away for two,
amid terrific cheers. Two to tie, three to win!

The next ball he snicked luckily for one. More cheers.
One to tie, two to win! The excitement was too terrible.
Men's hearts left their assigned quarters and climbed up

into throats and even mouths. Total strangers gripped
their neighbours' arms and legs with the force of a vice.
Even Mr Hornby, seasoned as he was to the game's vicis-
situdes and emotions, breathed in short gasps.

Mr Bettesworth had now to play. Every eye was on
him. The Gentlemen's faction thought, If only he can get
one and collar the over we are saved! The Players' sym-
pathizers thought, Please Heaven he's either bowled or
makes nothing! For Mr Bettesworth was more to be
trusted against Shaw than Mr Appleby was.

Amid another dead stillness Bates delivered the last ball
of the over, and Mr Bettesworth played it carefully.

A huge sigh swept the Pavilion. Respite at any rate.

The fieldsmen again changed places with cynical
deliberateness, and again Mr Appleby prepared to bat.
Everything depended upon the next moment.

Alfred Shaw, fondling the ball, looked thoughtfully
down his long shrewd nose. Then he altered the field a
little. He was laying a trap.

"Now, Arthur, you must look out," muttered Mr
Hornby despairingly.

One to tie, two to win!

Mr Appleby glanced carelessly to the Pavilion. If anyone could carry the thing through by sheer want of
nerves it was he.

Shaw now was ready. He took his little run, moved his
arm with its beautiful easy rhythm, and delivered a ball
which apparently had no other purpose than to be hit for
six. Mr Appleby made to hit it, realized that it was shorter
than he thought, and sweetly and simply put it back into
Shaw's hands.

The match was over; the Players had won by one
run! . . .

In the scene of confusion which followed, Mr Hornby disappeared and Rudd was lost among big men shouting and clapping. . . .

Gradually the ground emptied. But Rudd could not go yet, for he had lost a bet, and must settle it. His only penny was held tightly in a hot hand as he watched the door by which the Gentlemen came out. One by one they emerged, and at last came his hero, carrying his cricket bag and accompanied by three or four others, all talking and laughing. For the first time Rudd saw him wearing a hat.

Many a boy would have gone up to him and said, "Here's your penny," but Rudd could not break into the conversation. He must keep close and wait for his chance. They all walked slowly down to the gate where the cabs waited, Rudd at their heels. There they got into a cab.

Rudd stood by, looking earnestly at the great man and hoping for a glance of recognition, but it never came; and off went the cab.

Amid so much excitement how could a captain of Gentlemen remember a penny? Rudd realized that: but how he would have liked to pay!

It was not only the first bet he ever made, but the only bet he ever made to a forgetful winner.

Landmarks.   1914

RODERICK'S PRO'S

[A Story for Boys]

ONCE upon a time there was a little boy of ten, who bowled out C. B. Fry. This little boy's name was Roderick Bulstrode (or Bulstrode is the name that we will give him here), and he lived in St. John's Wood, in one of the houses whose gardens join Lord's. His father played for the M.C.C. a good deal, and practised in the nets almost every day, to the bowling of various professionals, or pro's, as they are called for short, but chiefly to that of Tom Stick; and in the summer Roderick was more often at Lord's than not.

How it came about that Roderick bowled C. B. Fry was this way. Middlesex were playing Sussex, and Mr Fry went to the nets early to practise, and Roderick's father bowled to him and let Roderick have the ball now and then. And whether it was that Mr Fry was not thinking, or was looking another way, or was simply very good-natured, I don't know, but one of Roderick's sneaks got under his bat and hit the stumps. (They were not sneaks, you must understand, because he wanted to bowl sneaks, but because he was not big enough to bowl any other way for 22 yards. He was only ten.) Roderick thus did that day what no one else could do, for Mr Fry went in and made 143 not out, in spite of all the efforts of Albert Trott and Tarrant and J. T. Hearne.

Roderick's bedroom walls had been covered with portraits of cricketers for years, but after he bowled out C. B. Fry he took away a lot of them and made an open space with the last picture postcard of Mr Fry right in the middle of it, and underneath, on the mantelpiece, he put the ball he had bowled him with, which his father gave him, under a glass shade. And other little St John's Wood boys, friends of Roderick's from the Abbey Road, and Hamilton Terrace, and Loudoun Road, and that very attractive red-brick village with a green of its own just off the Avenue Road, used to come and see it, and stand in front of it and hold their breath, rather like little girls looking at a new baby.

Roderick also had a "Cricketers' Birthday Book", so that when he came down to breakfast he used to say, "Tyldesley's thirty-five to-day," "Hutchings is twenty-four," and so on. And he knew the initials of every first-class amateur and the Christian name of every pro.

That was not Roderick's only cricketing triumph. It is true that he had never succeeded in bowling out any other really swell batsman, but he had shaken hands with Sammy Woods and J. R. Mason, and one day Lord Hawke took him by both shoulders and lifted him to one side, saying: "Now then, Tommy, out of the way." But these were only chance acquaintances. His real cricketing friend was Tom Stick, the ground bowler.

Tom Stick came from Devonshire, which is a county without a first-class eleven that plays the M.C.C. in August, and he lived in a little street off Lisson Grove, where he kept a bird-fancier's shop. For most professional cricketers, you know, are something else as well, or they would not be able to live in the winter. Many of them make cricket-bats, many keep inns, many are gardeners. I know one who is a picture-framer, and another an organist, while George Hirst, who is the greatest of them all, makes toffee. Well, Tom Stick was a bird-fancier, with a partner named Dick Crawley, who used to mind the shop when Tom had to be at Lord's bowling to gentlemen, Roderick's father

L

among them, or playing against Haileybury or Rugby or wherever he was sent to do all the hard work and go in last.

Roderick's father was very fond of Tom and was quite happy to know that Roderick was with him, so that Roderick not only used to join Tom at Lord's, but also at the shop off Lisson Grove, where he often helped in cleaning out the cages and feeding the birds and teaching the bullfinches to whistle, and was very good friends also with certain puppies and rabbits. His own dog, a fox-terrier named "Sinhji", had come from Tom.

Tom used to bowl to Roderick in the mornings before the gentlemen arrived for their practice, and he taught him to hold his bat straight and not slope it, and to keep his feet still and not draw them away when the ball was coming (which are the two most important things in batting), and it was he who stopped Roderick from carrying an autograph-book about and worrying the cricketers for their signatures. In fact, Tom was a kind of nurse to Roderick, and they were so much together that, whereas Tom was known to Roderick's small friends as "Roddy's Pro", Roderick was known to Tom's friends as "Sticky's Shadow".

Now it happened that last summer Roderick's father had been making a great many runs for the M.C.C. in one of their tours. (Roderick did not see him, for he had to stay at home and do his lessons; but his father sent him a telegram after each innings.) Mr Bulstrode (as we are calling him) batted so well, indeed, that when he returned to London he was asked to play for Middlesex against Yorkshire on the following Monday, to take the place of one of the regular eleven who was ill; and you may be sure he said yes, for, although he was now thirty-two, this was the first time he had ever been asked to play for his county.

Roderick, you may be equally sure, was also pleased; and when his father suddenly said to him, "Would you like to come with me?" his excitement was almost too great to bear.

"And Tom too?" he asked, after a minute or so.

"Yes, Tom's going," said his father. "He's going to field if anyone is hurt or has to leave early. But if he's not wanted he will look after you."

"Hurray!" said Roderick. "I know what I shall do. I shall score every run and keep the bowling analysis too."

The train left St Pancras on the Sunday afternoon, and that in itself was an excitement, for Roderick had never travelled on Sunday before; but before that had come the rapture of packing his bag, which on this occasion was not an ordinary one, but an old cricket-bag of his father's, which he begged for, in which were not only his sponge and collars and other necessary things, but his flannels and his bat and pads.

This bag he insisted upon carrying himself all along the platform, and, as several of the Middlesex team were also on their way to the train at the same moment, the presence of so small a cricketer in their midst made a great sensation among the porters.

"My word!" said one, "Yorkshire will have to look out this time."

"Who's the giant," asked another, "walking just behind Albert Trott? I shouldn't like to be in when he bowled his fastest."

But Roderick was unconscious of any laughter. He was the proudest boy in London, although his arm, it is true, was beginning to ache horribly. But when, as he was climbing into the carriage, the guard lifted him up and called him "Prince Run-get-simply", he joined in the fun.

It was a deliriously happy journey, for all the cricketers were very nice to him, and Mr Warner talked about Australia, and Mr Bosanquet showed him how he held the ball to make it break from the leg when the batsman thought it was going to break from the off, and at Nottingham Mr Douglas bought him a bun and a banana. They got to Sheffield just before eight, and Roderick went to bed very soon after, in a little bed in his father's room in the hotel.

The first thing Roderick did the next morning was to buy a scoring-book and a pencil, and then he and his father explored Sheffield a little before it was time to go to the ground at Bramall Lane and get some practice.

The people clustered all round and in front of the nets and watched the batsmen, and now and then they were nearly killed, as always happens before a match. They pointed out the cricketers to each other.

"There's Warner," they said. "That's Bosanquet—the tall one." "Where's Trott? Why, there, bowling at Warner. Good old Alberto!" and so on.

"Who's the man in the end net?" Roderick heard some one ask.

"I don't know. One of Middlesex's many new men, I suppose," said the other.

"But he can hit a bit, can't he?" the first man said, as Roderick's father stepped out to a ball and banged it half-way across the ground.

Roderick was very proud, and he felt that the time had come to make his father known. "That's Bulstrode," he said.

"Oh, that's Bulstrode, is it?" said the second man. "I've heard of him. He makes lots of runs on the M.C.C. tours. But I guess Georgy'll get him."

"Who is Georgy?" asked Roderick.

"Georgy—why, where do you come from? Fancy being in Sheffield and asking who Georgy is. Georgy is Georgy Hirst, of course."

Roderick walked back to the pavilion with his father very proudly. "You'll have to be very careful how you play Hirst," he said.

"I shall," said his father; "but why?"

"Because the men were saying he's going to get you." Mr Bulstrode laughed; but he thought it very likely too.

I'm not going to tell you all about the match, for it lasted three days, and was very much like other matches. Roderick had a corner seat in the pavilion, where he could see everything, and for the first day he scored every run and kept the analysis right through. This included his father's innings, which lasted, alas! far too short a time, for, after making four good hits to the boundary, he was caught close in at what was called silly mid-on, off—what bowler do you think?—George Hirst.

But the next day Roderick gave up work, because he wanted to see more of Tom, and Tom made room for him in the professionals' box while Yorkshire were in, and he saw all the wonderful men—quite close too—Tunnicliffe and Denton and Hirst—and even talked with them. Hirst sat right in front of the box, with his brown sunburned arms on the ledge, and his square, jolly, sunburned face on his arms, and said funny things about the play in broad Yorkshire; and now and then he would say something to Roderick. And then suddenly down went a wicket, and Hirst got up to go in.

"Give me a wish for luck," he said to Roddy.

"I wish my father may catch you out," said Roddy; "but not until," he added, "you have made a lot of runs."

"If he does," said Hirst, "I'll give thee some practice to-morrow morning."

Poor Roddy, this was almost too much. It is bad enough to watch your favourites batting at any time, for every ball may be the last; but it is terrible when you equally want two people to bring something off—for Roddy wanted Hirst (whom he now adored) to make a good innings, and, at the same time, he wanted his father to catch Hirst out.

Hirst was not out when it was time for lunch, and so Roderick was able to tell his father all about it.

"What's this, Hirst?" said Mr Bulstrode, when the teams were being photographed. "Give me a chance, and let me see if I can hold it."

Hirst laughed, and when he laughs it is like a sunset in fine weather. "I have a spy round to see where thee're standing every over," he said, "and that's where I'll never knock it."

"But what about my boy's practice?" Mr Bulstrode replied.

"Ah, we'll see about that," said the Yorkshireman.

But, as a matter of fact, Roderick got his practice according to the bargain, for, as it happened, it was Mr Bulstrode who caught Hirst, at third man.

I need hardly tell you that Roderick dreamed that night. His sleep was full of Hirsts, all jolly and all hitting catches which his father buttered. But in the morning, when he knew how true his luck was, he was almost too happy. Hirst was as good as his word, and they practised in the nets together for nearly half an hour, and Roderick nearly bowled him twice.

In Middlesex's next innings Roderick's father made thirty-five, all of which Roderick scored with the greatest care; but the match could not be finished owing to a very heavy shower, and so this innings did not matter very much one way or the other, except that it made Mr Bulstrode's place safe for another match.

Of that match I am not going to tell; but I have perhaps said enough to show you how exceedingly delightful it must be to have a father who plays for his county.

Anne's Terrible Good Nature.   1913

THE DARK SECRET

I⊤ was the most perfect September day that anyone could remember. The sun had risen in a dewy mist. The early air was pungent with yellowing bracken.

Then the mist cleared, the dew disappeared from everywhere but the shadows, and the Red Admirals again settled on the Michaelmas daisies.

A young man walked up and down the paths of the garden and drank in its sweetness; then he passed on to the orchard and picked from the wet grass a reddening apple, which he ate. Something pulled at his flannel trousers: it was a spaniel puppy, and with it he played till breakfast-time.

He was staying with some friends for a cricket match. It was the last of the season and his only game that year. As one grows older and busier, cricket becomes less and less convenient, and on the two occasions that he had arranged for a day it had been wet.

He had never been a great hand at the game. He had never made 100 or even 70, never taken any really good wickets; but he liked every minute of a match, so much so that he was always the first to volunteer when there was a man short, or run for some one who was lame, or even to stand as umpire.

To be in the field was the thing. Those rainy interludes in the pavilion which so develop the stoicism of the first-class cricketer had no power to make a philosopher of him. All their effect on him was detrimental: they turned him black. He fretted and raged.

But to-day there was not a cloud; nothing but the golden September sun.

168

It was one of the jolly matches. There was no jarring element: no bowler who was several sizes too good; no bowler who resented being taken off; no habitual country-house cricketer whose whole conversation was the jargon of the game; no batsman too superior to the rest; no acerbitous captain with a lost temper over every mistake; no champagne for lunch. Most of the players were very occasional performers: the rest were gardeners and a few schoolboys. Nice boys—boys who might have come from Winchester.

He was quickly out, but he did not mind, for he had had one glorious swipe and was caught in the deep field off another, and there is no better way of getting out than that.

In the field he himself stood deep, and the only catch that came to him he held; while in the intervals between wickets he lay on the sweet grass while the sun warmed him through and through. If ever it was good to be alive. . . .

And suddenly the sun no longer warmed him, and he noticed that it had sunk behind a tree in whose hundred-yard-long shadow he was standing. For a second he shivered, not only at the loss of tangible heat, but at the realization that the summer was nearly gone (for it was still early in the afternoon), and this was the last cricket match, and he had missed all the others, and he was growing old, and winter was coming on, and next year he might have no chance; but most of all he regretted the loss of the incredible goodness of this day, and for the first time in his life the thought phrased itself in his mind: "No sooner do we grasp the present than it becomes the past." The haste of it all oppressed him. Nothing stands still.

"A ripping day, wasn't it?" said his host as they walked back.

"Perfect," he replied with a sigh. "But how soon over!"

They stopped for a moment at the top of the hill to look at the sunset, and he sighed again as his thoughts flew to that print of the "Melancholia" which had hung on the stairs in his early home.

"Notice the sunset," some visitor had once said to him. "Some day you will know why Dürer put that in."

And now he knew.

That evening he heard the Winchester boys making plans for the winter sports at Pontresina in the Christmas vac.

A Boswell of Bagdad.   1917

VIEWS IN VERSE

All this section comes from *Willow and Leather*.   1898

THE GAME

THE winds and the rains of the winter are done,
And lo! in the sky the beneficent sun,
The pitch is close-shaven and firm for our tread,
There's a thrush on the bough and a lark overhead.
 So, cricketers all,
 Hark, hark to the call!—
And on with your flannels and into the field,
The leather to grasp and the willow to wield.

Now croquet is only for couples who spoon,
And football is wintry, and over too soon;
Lawn tennis for girls and to fill up odd time,
And golf for old buffers who're out of their prime.
 But cricket, in truth,
 Is for youth, is for youth!
For frames that are hardy and hearts that are light,
For feet that are nimble and muscles of might.

The bat has had heroes as great as the sword:
Beldham and Lambert and Aylward and Ward,
Pilch and Mynn, Carpenter, Thornton and Parr—
These were the stalwarts to speed the ball far;
 But great though they be,
 To W.G.
The greatest among them must ever give place:
To mighty, transcendent, unparalleled Grace!

The little red ball has had masters of mark:
Harris and Lumpy and Hillyer and Clarke,

"Lilly" the elder, the great "Nonpareil",
Alfred Shaw, Richardson, Spofforth and Steel.
    These are but few
    Of the good men and true
Whose fingers have lent such a deuce to the ball,
That Willow, proud Willow, has had to sing small!

A word for the umpires, who stand the long day,
Good fellows, who give us the blessed word "Play!"
A word for the scorers, whose fingers record
For joy of the future our deeds on the sward;
    And one for the lads
    In gauntlets and pads
Who, ruling (like Charon of old) o'er the sticks,
Get few of the halfpence and most of the kicks.[1]

O think of the joy as your fingers close round
The leather, slogged high to the end of the ground!
O think of the music there is in the shout
Proclaiming at last that a blocker is out!
    O think of the cheer,
    In a tankard of beer,
Of the notable goodness of salad and beef,
Of the warmth of the sun, of the green of the leaf!

[1] Wicket-keepers of to-day can show battered fists enough; but in the early years of the game their hands came in for woeful punishment. It was then the stumper's duty to pop the ball (hence "popping" crease) into a hole between the two wickets before the striker's club could be grounded there. Often and often the club and the hand reached the spot at the same moment. "The fingers of an old cricketer," wrote Mr Mitford, "so scarred, so bent, so shattered, so indented, so contorted, so venerable! are enough to bring tears of envy and emulation from any eye,—*we* are acquainted with *such a pair of hands,* 'if hands they may be called, that shape have none!' " But wounds did not deter those heroic, unprotected men. "We never thought of knocks," said Beldham to Mr Pycroft in 1837. [E.V.L.]

'Tis our national game, and it still will hold sway,
As much twenty thousand years hence as to-day:
Young England will ever desire with its soul
Big biceps to hit with, shrewd fingers to bowl.
    And where'er you may be
    'Neath the Jack flying free,
Some Briton you'll light on whose dearest of hopes
Is to bang a full-pitcher clean over the ropes.

GOOD DAYS

WILLOW and cane, nothing but that—
O, but it's glorious, swinging the bat!
Leather and thread, there you have all—
O, but it's glorious, gripping the ball!
Grass at our feet, and the sun overhead,
Here let us play till the evening is red.
Then to our dinner, and lustily sing,
Cricket's the King of games, Cricket is King!

THE SONG OF THE BALL

LEATHER—the heart o' me, leather—the rind o' me,
    O but the soul of me's other than that!
Else, should I thrill as I do so exultingly
    Climbing the air from the thick o' the bat?

Leather—the heart o' me: ay, but in verity
   Kindred I claim with the sun in the sky.
Heroes, bow all to the little red ball,
   And bow to my brother ball blazing on high.

     Pour on us torrents of light, good sun,
       Shine in the hearts of my cricketers, shine;
     Fill them with gladness and might, good sun,
       Touch them with glory, O brother of mine,
         Brother of mine,
         Brother of mine!
     We are the lords of them, brother and mate,
     I but a little ball, thou such a great !

Give me the bowler whose fingers embracing me
   Tingle and throb with the joy of the game,
One who can laugh at a smack to the boundary,
   Single of purpose and steady of aim.
That is the man for me: striving in sympathy,
   Ours is a fellowship sure to prevail.
Willow must fall in the end to the ball—
   See, like a tiger I leap for the bail!

Give me the fieldsman whose eyes never stray from me,
   Eager to clutch me, a roebuck in pace:
Perish the unalert, perish the "buttery",
   Perish the laggard I strip in the race.
Grand is the ecstasy, soaring triumphantly,
   Holding the gaze of the meadow is grand,
Grandest of all to the soul of the ball
   Is the finishing grip of the honest brown hand.

Give me the batsman who squanders his force on me,
  Crowding the strength of his soul in a stroke:
Perish the muff and the little-tin-Shrewsbury,
  Meanly contented to potter and poke.
He who would pleasure me, he must do doughtily,—
  Bruises and buffetings stir me like wine.[1]
Giants, come all, do your worst with the ball,
  Sooner or later you're mine, sirs, you're mine!

        Pour on us torrents of light, good sun,
          Shine in the hearts of my cricketers, shine,
        Fill them with gladness and might, good sun,
          Touch them with glory, O brother of mine,
              Brother of mine,
              Brother of mine!
        We are the lords of them, brother and mate:
        I but a little ball, thou such a great! [2]

LOVE IN THE MEADOW

The Bat sings:
"My love is red as a damask rose,
    And lovers true are we,
Though ever I strive to belabour her,
    And she to outwit me;

[1] In a moving little story in *Chambers' Journal*, entitled *A Bowler's Innings*, by Mr E. W. Hornung, I find this contradictory sentiment: "Ay, there's a deal o' human natur' in a treble-seam, sir; it don't like getting knocked about any more than we do." [E.V.L.]

[2] I am proud to say that when Sir Herbert Baker, Lutyens's colleague in the building of the New Delhi, designed the new gates for Lord's as a memorial to W. G. Grace, he took, he tells me, the idea of the sun and the cricket ball from these verses of mine. [E.V.L. in *Reading, Writing and Remembering*, 1932.]

M

And yet alone we pine and moan,
  We cannot rejoice at all,
For what is a ball without a bat,
  Or a bat without a ball?

"We never embrace but we often kiss,
  We only meet to part;
The farther away I speed my love,
  The gladder I am at heart;
And glad is she to torture me,
  Gladder to see me fall,
Yet great is the love of the ball for the bat
  And the love of the bat for the ball!

"Her skin is rough as a Ribston red,
  Her heart is O so hard!
And enemy-like she plots and plans
  To catch me off my guard;
Yet she is the only love I love,
  And I am her all in all;
And stranger thing on the earth's not seen
  Than the marriage of bat and ball."

DRIVING TO THE MATCH

THE linnets flit from hedge to hedge,
  The lark exults on high,
The cattle, crowded at the brook,
Lift up their dripping heads to look
  As we go driving by.

The hoofs are on the road, boys,
    They ring a merry catch:
O the sun's at noon and the year's at June,
    And we're driving to the match!

The brown-armed peasants in the hay
    Stand still with shaded eye,
The village children shout with glee,
And mothers leave their work to see
    As we go driving by.

The milkmaid flings a saucy smile,
    The farmer heaves a sigh,
Our horses' music floods the air,
And all the world is O so fair
    As we go driving by!

The hoofs are on the road, boys,
    Hark to their jocund catch:
O the sun's at noon and the year's at June,
    And we're driving to the match!

ECSTASY

TWENTY-TWO Englishmen, blithesome and vigorous,
    On with your flannels, and haste to the game;
Greet the Earth-Mother, and meet the sun face to face,
    Offer your brows for the kiss of his flame!
Children of Midsummer, Sons of the Open Air,
    Here in this meadow, this fair summer day,
Here 'mid the song o' birds, here 'mid the hum o' noon,
    Here will we play!

Is there a braver sight, say, in the universe?
  Match me, you painter, this scene for a pound—
Over our meadow the hazy blue firmament,
  Shadows of purple on emerald ground.
Then, scattered near and far, see the bright warriors,
  Stout of heart, clean of limb, steady of eye;
Health is our Goddess, and nobly we worship her,
          'Neath the clear sky.

See how the flashing bat thrashes the careless ones!
  Mark how the stalwarts spring over the turf!
Hear the flushed veterans living brave days again,
  Down in the cider-tent white as the surf!
Hark, how the lusty palms beat exultation out!
  Scorer, old fellow, your fingers grow sore!
Listen, three cheers, English cheers, for the conquerors!
          Listen, three more!

RHAPSODY

O TO face swift bowling
  On a perfect wicket,
    'Mid eleven foemen
      Bent upon one's flight!
He who's poured his soul in
  Hero-kindling Cricket—
    He has lived his moment,
      He has plumbed delight!

Men may seek emotions,
Taste them by the million;
But—to leap to meet her,
Meet the flying ball,
Grandly then to lift her
Over the pavilion,
Gives a thrill that's sweeter,
Sweeter than them all!

THAT BAT![1]

The Veteran Speaks:

SUCH a bat! such a bat!
Full many a bat have I wielded since then,
And cut with, and driven with, time and again,
But never a one like that!

The handle was thin, with a cane or two split,
And it whipped in the grip when one made a full hit,
While every particle thrilled;
And the thick of the blade wore a band of black thread
As bracing, or, if you prefer it instead,
As a mark of respect for good balls that were dead,
Good balls it had jumped for and killed.

There are bats of all kinds, as you cricketers know,
The few to be played with, the many for show.
And some that will drive are too heavy for cutting,
And some that will cut are at driving no go;

[1] I wish I could claim this experience for my own. [E.V.L.]

And some block a yorker as if it were nothing,
While some sting you up if you tap at a slow.
There are bats of all kinds, 'twixt the best and the worst,
And mine, though it looked like a ruin, was first!

O, a hop to the off is a joy and delight,
And a full-pitch to leg it is glory to smite,
But a simple half-volley is finest, I tell you, is finest of
    all!
And cheering it was when the winter was here,
And the sulky rain dripped and the heavens were drear,
To pick up my bat from its place by the wall,
And poise it, and swing it, and throb to recall
How 'twould leap in my hand to be hitting that ball,
That simple half-volley, the finest, I tell you, the finest of
    all.

Though never so tenderly after its toil
You lay it away with a dressing of oil,
A bat suffers much in a drought.

And so it befell that one August in Kent,
Where the pitch burnt your feet, and was hard as cement,
And the brows of the fieldsmen were darklingly bent
Because we would never get out—
(Though shandy-gaff foamed in the cool of the tent
We wouldn't, we couldn't, get out)—
I heard a sharp crack at our twenty-first four,
And half of the blade flew away to mid-wicket;
And half of the zest vanished ever from cricket,
And the day of my Beauty was o'er.

Such a bat! such a bat!
Full many a bat have I handled since then,
And cut with, and driven with, time and again,
But never a one like that.
Thrice happy the ghost who the ghost of it wields—
Such joy must be his in Elysian fields!

A REFLECTION

WHEN first I learned to bat,
    A man devoid of luck—
His innings done without a run—
    Had made, we said, a "duck".

But now the word is changed;
    And he who, with a sob,
Comes back before he helps the score,
    Has made, we say, a "blob".

(A "blob" I can't derive;
    But "duck", of course you know,
Means egg, because, by Nature's laws,
    An egg is like an O.)

But still, whatever name
    We choose (I've often thought),
The fact remains, with all our pains,
    A nought is still a nought.

THE POINT OF VIEW

"The game of cricket has also done much for England in bringing the upper and lower classes together." Lord Harris, speaking at Stratford.

The Hon. SLOGLEY BATT, *loq*:

" 'BRINGS us together?' Why, truly,
    But parts us uncommonly soon;
I was thought the best man, I remember,
    In a match down in Surrey last June.
We were playing a bloomin' village,
    They were labourers, every Jack,
And they put on a blacksmith Johnnie
    To open the bowlin' attack.
I wanted to stay for a fortnight . . .
    I went in a minute or less,
With a duck to my name and a feelin' of shame,
    For he bowled like a bally express."

BILL SWIPES, *loq*:

" 'Brings us together!' but often
    I'm blowed if it does much more!
I remember a match last summer,
    I backed myself for a score.
We were playing a team of nobs, sir,
    As swagger a lot as you'll see;
And I thought as I looked 'em over,
    I'm in for a fair old spree. . . .
I jumped for the first half-volley,
    My aunt! how the leather went,
But a blanky young toff what was fielding mid-off,
    He bustled me back to the tent.

HOME AND AWAY

THE BATS

THERE is a street in London called Cranbourn Street, which serves no particular purpose of its own, but is useful as leading from Long Acre and Garrick Street to the frivolous delights of the Hippodrome, and serviceable also in the possession of a Tube station from which one may go to districts of London as diverse as Golder's Green and Hammersmith. These to the ordinary eye are the principal merits of Cranbourn Street. But, to the eye which more minutely discerns, it has deeper and finer treasure: it has a shop window with a little row of cricket bats in it so discreetly chosen that they not only form a vivid sketch of the history of the greatest of games but enable anyone standing at the window and studying them to defeat for the moment the attack of the dreariest of weather and for a brief but glorious space believe in the sun again.

And what of the treasures? Well, to begin with, the oldest known bat is there—a dark lop-sided club such as you see in the early pictures in the pavilion of Lord's, that art gallery which almost justifies rain during a match, since it is only when rain falls that one examines it with any care. Of this bat there is obviously no history, or it would be written upon it, and the fancy is therefore free to place it in whatever hands one will—Tom Walker's, or Beldham's, or Lord Frederick Beauclerk's, or even Richard Nyren's himself, father of the first great eulogist of the game. Beside it is another veteran, not quite so old, though, and approaching in shape the bat of our own day—such a bat as Lambert, or that dauntless sportsman, Mr Osbaldeston ("The Squire," as he was known in the hunting-field), may have swung in one of their famous single-wicket contests.

Beside these is even more of a curiosity. Nothing less than the very bat which during his brief and not too glorious cricket career was employed to defend his wicket, if not actually to make runs, by the late King Edward VII when he was Prince of Wales. For that otherwise accomplished ruler and full man (as the old phrase has it) was never much of a C. B. Fry. He knew the world as few have known it; he commanded respect and affection; he was accustomed to give orders and have them instantly obeyed; but almost anyone could bowl him out, and it is on record that those royal hands, so capable in their grasp of orb and sceptre, had only the most rudimentary and incomplete idea of retaining a catch. Such are human limitations! Here, however, in the Cranbourn Street window, is His Majesty's bat, and even without the accompanying label one would guess that it was the property of no very efficient cricketer. For it lacks body; no one who really knew would have borne to the pitch a blade so obviously incapable of getting the ball to the ropes; while just beneath the too fanciful splice is a silver plate. Now all cricketers are aware that it is when the incoming man carries a bat with a silver plate on it that the scorers (if ever) feel entitled to dip below the table for the bottle and glass and generally relax a little.

So much for what may be called the freaks of this fascinating window. Now for the facts. A very striking fact indeed is the splintered bat with which Mr G. L. Jessop made a trifle of 168 against Lancashire. I wish the date was given; I wish even more that the length of the innings in minutes was given. Whether the splinters were lost then, or later, we should also be told. But there it is, and, after seeing it, how to get through these infernal months of February and March and April and half May, until real life begins again, one doesn't know and can hardly conjecture. And what do you think is beside it? Nothing less than "the best bat" that Mr M. A. Noble ever played with—the leisurely, watchful Australian master, astute captain, inspired change-bowler, and the steady, remorseless compiler of scores at the right time. It is something to have in darkest February Noble's best bat beneath one's eyes.

And lastly, there is a scarred and discoloured blade which bears the brave news that with it did that old man hirsute, now on great match-days a landmark in the Lord's pavilion, surveying the turf where once he ruled—W.G. himself, no less—make over a thousand runs. Historic wood, if you like; historic window!

No wonder, then, that I scheme to get Cranbourn Street into my London peregrinations. For here is youth renewed and the dismallest of winters momentarily slain.

Loiterer's Harvest. 1913

CRICKET N.B.

THE announcement that the author of *A Window in Thrums* was presenting his birthplace, Kirriemuir, with a cricket pavilion may have led to a little surprise, because cricket and Scotland are not much associated in our minds. We know that those hardy invaders are apt at golf, which has even been called Scotch croquet, and that they can curl, and toss the caber, and often play Rugby too well for the Southerner; but on its northern progress village cricket, in the uninstructed mind's-eye, stops at Yorkshire. The famous Scotch figures whom every follower of the game must be able to recall—such as, to name at the moment only two or three, the superb Gregor McGregor, who kept wicket for Cambridge, for Middlesex, for the Gentlemen, and for England; and the light-hearted Nigel Haig, who does so much to bring cheerfulness to Lord's to-day—these we have supposed learned their cricket at schools or universities south of the Tweed. Among my own early recollections is the polished batting of J. M. Cotterill, who came from Scotland to play for Sussex. But such isolated cases have never led us to think that Scotland was a nursery of the game. For how should Caledonia stern and wild prepare pitches? we ask ourselves. Yet we are wrong! Scotland has many a sward where runs may be made, and in Forfarshire they are particularly keen, and Sir James Barrie (whose slow lefts used to be very effective) has again had an inspiration.

The sporadic character of first-class cricket has always been rather puzzling to me, and not less so since the invention of the motor-car has made it possible to see so much of England. There is good reason why Cumberland

and Westmorland should not be too friendly to the game, because they are mountainous and attract rain. Rutland, of course, notoriously has not room for a cricket ground. Shropshire and Herefordshire are hilly. Devonshire gives way too much to a passion for moors. But why cannot eleven players of first-class quality be trained on the level meads of Wiltshire and Dorset, Berkshire and Oxfordshire, Hertfordshire and Huntingdonshire, Bedfordshire and Cambridgeshire, Suffolk and Norfolk? This is a great mystery. One does not want them necessarily to play all the other counties; one wants to know why cricket should be less ardently pursued in one county favourable to it than in another. One wants to know why the tide left a county. Did Norfolk's interest in cricket die with Fuller Pilch? Was it because there were no more Carpenters and Haywards that Cambridgeshire cooled?

To return to Scotland, it chances that at the same time that I read about Sir James Barrie's pavilion I received a handsome book, which must be said to settle, once and for all, the question whether or not the Scots are cricketers, for it is entitled *Annals of Brechin Cricket, 1849–1927*, written by Mr Alfred O'Neill (whose name is to be found in the scores for many years), with a foreword by the Earl of Strathmore and Kinghorne. Brechin, like Kirriemuir, its ancient enemy, is in Forfarshire, which is a long way north, and the club has provided three international players in Douglas Ferrier, one of several distinguished brothers, W. Eddie and J. W. Sorrie. The great name of L. M. Balfour-Melville occurs often in the book as an antagonist of the Brechiners, playing for the Glamis Castle eleven, all among the Lyons. The Lord Glamis of those days, now the Earl of Strathmore, was once congratulated by a stuttering labourer, during the interval, in these cordial terms:

"Yi'rr a-a bloo-o-min' fi-fi-fine b-b-ooler, Maister Glamis. Yi did rael weel th'day." A story that is usually associated with our own W.G is here told about the W.G. of Scotland, as Balfour-Melville was called: how he was given not out l.b.w. from the first ball he received, and stayed in to make 99. "But surely he was out?" someone afterwards asked the umpire, Dr Anderson. "Of course he was," said the doctor, "but I'd never seen him bat." A contemporary of this far from upright though very human judge was the Brechiner, James Adam, who had a deadly yorker. "Sharp as a needle in the field," writes the historian, "ever with a jaunty step and smiling face, he was verily the sunshine of cricket." It was not, however, a Brechiner but Peter Lindsay, the Kirriemuir all-rounder, who does the most remarkable thing in the book, for once, even after he had become a veteran, he took six wickets with six consecutive balls.

That Scotland could be interested in our national game as far back as 1849 we find from an account of a match in the *Montrose Standard*, where we have such reportorial tropes as these:

"Martin joined Sir James, but had no sooner taken his stand than he agreed to retire, at the urgent request of Rodgers, who shattered his nerves with a bailer. . . .

"Murray, after batting for a few minutes, 'with all the feeling and quaintness of past ages,' heard an ominous crash in the rear, and on turning round had his feelings so much shocked by the appearance of his stumps that he retired horrified for a one. . . .

"Sir James Baird, in attempting a severe hit off a full-pitched ball from Rodgers, struck it with the edge of his bat, which sent it into a purer atmosphere, a chance of which Smeaton availed himself."

But if it is a surprise to find that Scotland plays cricket

so much and that one small club can provide material for a portly volume, how will the news be received that a guide to cricket for Frenchmen has been published? A copy lies before me—*Le Cricket pour les Sportsmen Français* —by R. Macdonald Lucas (no nepotism is at work here). In this sprightly work, which, though serious in intention, is informed by a gay humour and which has some amusing pictures and diagrams, the whole game is set forth with such clearness that did he give his strenuous logical mind to it, M. Poincaré might be able to lead a team into the field against England. My namesake believes the game to be of the utmost antiquity—indeed, he has a drawing of a match in the Garden of Eden with Adam bowling, Eve batting, and the Serpent as umpire, while he uses a hypothetical match between Old Testament notabilities as his first example. In this struggle some very odd things occurred: Cain was out through handling the ball, Abel hit it twice, Moses obstructed the field, and Jonah's substitute was run out. Cain seems to have been the wicket-keeper. A copious vocabulary turns the old familiar phrases into the language of diplomacy. Thus: l.b.w. becomes *jambe-devant-guichet*, while this is the admirable definition of a yorker: "*Un service qui touche terre dans l'encoche faite par la batte—assez difficile à jouer! Un batteur qui s'avance peut la jouer à la volée—mais au risque d'être 'pris sorti'* [stumped] *par le garde-guichet, ou 'boulé', s'il la manque!*" Paris now has its Anglo-Franco contests regularly through the summer, and here again I fancy that Sir James Barrie is to some extent implicated, for I believe that a match between the *Peter Pan* company and some other team, organized by him twenty years ago, first drew the attention of many Parisians to the game.

Turning Things Over. 1929

N

LOST BALL!

"LOST Ball!" is now rarely cried in a big match, except of late years at Whitgift School, where a young gentleman named Crawford was continually making huge drives into the heart of Croydon, so that no citizen felt safe during the cricket season; but among those who play on commons, in meadows, and in exiguous back gardens, a lost ball makes a too frequent diversion. Much has been written of the malice of inanimate things, such as pencils, and collar-studs, and all the little toilet necessaries which so readily conceal themselves when they are most required, yet the malignancy of a cricket ball can beat them hollow. With the whole field to disport itself in, why does the ball take such joy in bounding over the fence, or seeking the innermost arcana of the brambles, or rolling into the ditch? Once or twice in an afternoon, and we should call it accident; but it occurs time and again, and there is no word left but malice.

Yet he is a good fellow, the treble-seam, and it goes hard to say anything against him; and when the loss comes in the midst of a good game, against his own wishes, you feel that he must feel the interruption as much as anybody. You picture him lying there, under a leaf or between the roots of ivy, or twenty feet from the nearest searcher, piteous in his impotence to attract eyes to his position. How a ball must sometimes long for speech!

Now and then the ball is not found at all at the first attempt. There are boys who get up before breakfast next morning to retrieve it. These boys are the salt of the earth. Other boys have the knack of finding a ball at once, like

194

Sherlock Holmes. They walk direct to the spot, sometimes
with their eyes shut, pause, and there it lies between their
boots. Others have recourse to magic. When Tom Sawyer
lost a marble in the woods and could not find it by diligent
search, he had resort to occult means.

"He went back to his treasure-house," says Mark Twain,
"and carefully placed himself just as he had been standing
when he tossed the marble away; then he took another
marble from his pocket and tossed it in the same way,
saying:
'Brother, go find your brother!'
He watched where it stopped, and went there and looked.
But it must have fallen short or gone too far, so he tried
twice more. The last repetition was successful. The two
marbles lay within a foot of each other."

All boys know this to be a tolerably sure device; but it is
easier with marbles than with cricket balls, because a boy
always has several marbles, but only one cricket ball.

In nine cases out of twelve a lost ball at cricket is found
at the moment the batsman reaches the spot. The nearest
fieldsman begins the hunt, then another and another join
him, languidly if the game has been proceeding for some
time, but zealously if it has only just begun. The bowler
and batsman stand where they are and shout instructions.
"A little more to the left." "Try just behind you." "It
went in a line with that tree." After a while, with a re-
proachful glance at the batsman, the bowler walks off.
The bowler begins by looking much nearer home than the
others; he does not want to flatter the batsman. At length,
very slowly, but with the air of one who cannot understand how others can be so dull and blind, the batsman
approaches the place, and when he is within a yard or two,

the ball is found. Why this should be so is inexplicable: it is one of Nature's conjuring tricks. But if not, if the trick fails, the batsman walks on far past the others before he deigns to look on the ground at all. Was it not he who hit the ball? In very hot weather a batsman often sees the ball sink into the brake fern with a sigh of relief. Uttering a hypocritical expression of regret, he flings himself on the ground, and the longer it is before the brake fern delivers up its secret the better he is pleased. Brake fern is, as a rule, very stubborn about this secret, but in no place does one hunt for a ball with more compensations, so sweet and rich and unmatchable is the scent of the bruised fronds.

While brake fern is the pleasantest, a thicket is the worst place in which to hunt a ball. The composition of the English thicket is five-eighths blackberry, two-eighths thorn, and one-eighth stinging-nettle. The question, "What *is* the good of stinging-nettles?" which everyone has asked at one time or another, is never so pertinent as when a ball lies, probably, in the midst of them. But the most hopeless place in which to hit is a field of standing corn. With each step you tread down so many stalks; the distance at which the ball fell is so difficult to calculate; and you have to keep one eye alert for the farmer. Standing grass is bad, but not so bad as wheat.

You find strange things while looking for a lost ball: other balls lost long ago and only dimly remembered, young rabbits, field-mice, larks' nests in the grass, and thrushes' and blackbirds' in the brambles; and a thousand and one objects so exactly like a ball from a distance that you shout the glad news. Some boys are always giving false alarms. Other boys continually ask, "Have you got it?" "Have you found it?", as though anyone in his senses would stay in a thicket a moment longer than is necessary.

In some families a dog is trained to retrieve lost balls. In others, alack! the dog makes off with them during play. There are, of course, balls that no one can find, that never come to light again, but lie on, through the summer, through the autumn, surrounded by curious creeping life, alternately soaked by rain and blistered by the sun, until they swell and split and afford harbourage for ants or beetles, and so gradually fall to pieces and mingle with the soil.

Willow and Leather. 1898

LITTLE BOYS' CRICKET

IF you want to see cruciform cricket you must visit one of London's open spaces on Saturday afternoon. Parliament Hill Fields will do. For a while, standing on the edge of the ground, you will be conscious only of chaos; but after a while, when your eyes have learned to penetrate an atmosphere thick and darkened with cricket balls, cosmos will emerge. Not the cosmos of a county ground, but the cosmos of a County Council. Consider the precautions taken to ensure advantageous cricket at Lord's—the screen for the bowler's arm, the roped ring, the stoppage of the game if a Pavilion habitué disconcerts the batsman by twisting his moustache—and then note the contiguity of pitch and pitch, on this County Council sward. We marvel that a bird is able to identify its own nest; surely the birds that flit here from elm to elm must marvel that a fieldsman knows his own wicket.

"Cruciform" is, perhaps, an exaggeration, but the pitches do everything short of crossing; they lie side by side, like railway lines, in some cases so close together that a wide ball bowled by a bowler in match number one may take the middle stump of a batsman in match number two. They lie end on, like drain-pipes, sometimes with so little intervening space that the wicket-keeper in one game finds himself, when he stoops to take the ball, backing into the wicket-keeper in another. And yet matches are played out, and results more or less satisfactory are reached, and the list of extraordinary performances which a morning paper diligently prints is swollen. Most of the bowlers who now-

adays take six wickets in six balls, or all the wickets for no
runs, do so under County Council auspices. It is not only
the confusion, but also the ground, that helps them.
Mother Earth was not more kind to Antæus than she is to
these County Council "ground" bowlers.

Curiously, it is only the spectator of cruciform cricket
that is in serious danger. The players themselves, being far
too much interested in their own games, are not much hurt
—the same providence that protects the drunkard from
broken limbs and concussion of the brain seems to preserve
them—but among those who stand aside and look on, the
visitations of the ball are frequent and terrible. But here,
again, the ball seems to make a distinction, for it hits only
those who go continually in fear of being hit; the others,
the careless ones, it avoids. How and why it avoids them
is a problem, just as it is a problem to a cyclist how and
why when he has to pick his way through stones by day,
on traversing the same piece of road by night a few hours
later, he can ride straight on without a jolt.

In spite of an occasional rap on the head or shin, the
spectator will be wise to stick to his post, for cruciform
cricket throws as interesting a light on human nature as any
performance there is. Perhaps the best return is offered
by the little boys' games. Little boys differ from their
elders in being always free to play cricket on open spaces.
There are always enough of them refraining from school to
make up several matches, and one need not, therefore, wait
for Saturday afternoon to study them. You cannot visit
Parliament Hill at any daylight hour without finding scores
of little boys disporting themselves about the base of
that northern eminence. These are the little boys that
are both seen and heard, in defiance of all sound nursery
canons.

A few minutes' observation of their habits yields a number of facts. You will notice that all little boys bat exactly alike. Individual style is a later growth. The only intentional hit is to long-on, and any ball that cannot be coerced thither is accounted of no use. In the admirable phrase of Mr Edward Lyttelton, "a pull is the primitive hit of the natural man". Cutting comes much later; not until the performer is well into the teens, and not always then. Whether he that pulls has less joy than he that plays the classical game, the illustrious and venerable cricketer who is known as the "Coroner" can best say. He has tried both on occasion. Little boys do occasionally hit to leg, but rarely at the first attempt. They miss the ball the first time, and then pursue it and bring off the stroke. In adult cricket there is not time to do this. Nor is there always time in little boys' cricket, for some of them bowl quite fast. In the presence of a swift ball the batsman closes his eyes, which probably is the case with more grown-ups than would confess to it. Nor does the little boy instinctively hold his bat straight: that also, like the cut, though less difficult, being an artificial acquirement. Some men go through life with crooked bats and make runs against the best bowling.

In ordinary practice games, where nothing is at stake, to hold the bat is the supreme ambition of the little boy, and in order to attain this end, he sticks at no device. To him all is fair in cricket; and his conscience offers no opposition to a rapid invention of new laws that shall, by their damning appropriateness, put the protesting batsman to shame. Little boys, by the way, when at last convinced that they are out, do not lay down the bat or hand it to the new-comer: they fling it. Once out, all their interest in the game is apt to vanish. And when the dislodged batsman is also the owner of the bat or ball, the game is apt abruptly to cease altogether.[1]

Similarly, all little boys bowl alike, save that some are straighter (less wide) than others. If the County Council would stop juvenile over-arm on its open spaces, the cricket of ten years hence would benefit. The bowlers wear themselves out. The knowledge that one ball is better than another comes later; the young bowler's first perception of the weakness of the batsman has reference only to his courage. He is not slow to note that a swift ball is the cause of a shrinking away from the stumps, and consequently he bowls swiftlier and swiftlier. His discovery that pitch is also advantageously varied is coeval with that of the capabilities of the off-hit. Now and then a little boy is born who arrives at these truths early—W.G. could probably hit all round at a time when other children are teething—but these are the exceptions that prove the rule. To most of us it is permitted to acquire no science until boyhood gives place to youth. Little boys have very vague ideas about runs, alternating extreme rashness with extreme timidity; but this matters very little, since the fielders have equally vague ideas about returning the ball to the wicket. Little boys avoid catches as if the game was Association football.

Willow and Leather. 1898

---

[1] An old story goes to prove that this method of stopping a game is not altogether confined to the very young cricketer. It tells of a farmer who lent a field for a match and was bowled first ball. "Out!" said the other side to the motionless batsman. "Hout?" he cried in dismay. "Hout? Then hout you go from my field!" [E.V.L.]

LORD'S AND LADIES

WHEN Blue meets Blue the student of Lord's types is a little bewildered. His eyes are dazzled by the unfamiliar presence of fair ladies, who swarm around the ring, and, in the interval, all over the ground, like such a cloud of butterflies as one comes upon suddenly in a clear space in a wood on a hot August day. But none the less the types are there, hidden away maybe among summer fashions, pressed out from their accustomed places by this brightly hued, cheering, invading host. Where is the churl who would grumble at the presence of Beauty's Daughters at a cricket match? Let him come forward and be rebuked. True, they have hats that shut out yards of the pitch; true, their heads are so restless that it little avails him who sits behind to crane his neck either way; true, their use of the sunshade shows a lack of imaginative sympathy; true, they talk frivolously of the most serious deeds ever performed on the green spots of the earth. These things are so. But who will complain, especially now that the Laureate of the game, Mr Norman Gale, has endowed the ball with their own sex, and thus has given them an equal right with ourselves to patronise cricket? And is it not fitting that noble dames should smile upon a pastime whose champion is a Grace? And may not the knowledge that such eyes are upon them impel the cricketers to finer heroism? And where should ladies naturally resort if not to Lord's? Then let no one begrudge them the place they occupy on these three days.

There are three kinds of cricket-match girls: the girl who knows all about the game, who scores her brother's

runs and keeps his bowling analysis, and takes not her eyes
from the wickets while any play is to be seen; and the girl
who is in a state of interested bewilderment; and the girl
who watches the game with her back. The first is im-
patient of extraneous interferences; the second is not un-
grateful for a little diversion; the third seeks it. "Well
played!" says (with no uncertain voice) the girl who knows.
"Is that man in the nightgown a don?" asks the second,
pointing her parasol at the umpire. "I prefer Sarah Bern-
hardt to Duse, in *La Dame*," says the third. And they all
may seem adorable—to different men.

And squeezed between the fair invaders whom do we
see? Well, there are the two old clergymen engaged in
their annual gossip over old times, recalling earlier 'Varsity
matches—the Cambridge victory by two runs in '70, and
the Oxford victory by six in '75; and chuckling over the
feats of old College friends. And there are the young
curates feeling more than a touch of regret that their
College days are over, and not a little sorry that cricket and
the Cloth are not more interdependent, especially as Mr
Norman Gale—a mere poet at best!—has told the world
how he "bowled three curates once with three consecutive
balls." One thing is very certain, and that is that the bard's
victims were not their Reverences R. T. Thornton, W.
Rashleigh, and F. Meyrick-Jones of the county of Kent.
No poet, not even Mr Swinburne, could have done that.

Then we hear the loud-voiced young man who knows
one of the Cambridge team—"awfully decent fellow"—
but was lucklessly unable to accept his offer of a seat in the
Pavilion; and there is the other young man who, when
playing against one of the Oxford eleven a week or so ago,
bowled him for a duck. Then who can be unconscious of the
very fresh undergraduate who now meets some of his old

schoolfellows for the first time since he left? How good it is to watch him playing the man about town, talking grandly of the bull-dogs he has fought and the rags he has incepted, and pityingly of the trammels of school life! With what an air he leads the way to the bar to order drinks, and how godlike is his mien to the younger boys! "Can we ever bridge this gulf?" they think, gazing in rapture on his waistcoat.

Lastly, there is the Lord's bore. He is in great form to-day. He points to Mr Blank and says, "That's Fry"; and when Mr Dash makes a good stroke, he cries, "Well hit, Druce." Whenever a bump-ball is caught he claps his hands and calls "Out!" and whenever a man steps out to hit he remarks, "Ah! he's forcing the game." For the Lord's bore is as one who has feasted on cricket reports and stolen the scraps. He calls a half-volley a yorker, and if the batsman prefers to let a dangerous off-ball go by untouched, he cries, "Beat him, by George!" Moreover, the Lord's bore gives fully five comments to the over. But what matters it? Cricket is open to all.

A word more of Lord's ladies. Their hour of triumph is in the interval, and proudest among them then are those who walk with a Blue. Once, in days that are past, of all who shed radiance upon Lord's one was esteemed by the two universities above all others. And he who was curious to know who this enchantress was, had but to wait until the agitated whisper, running round the ring like a racing bicycle, reached him—"There's Maude Millett!" I know not who has taken her place.

Willow and Leather. 1898

THE MEDITERRANEAN GAME

"WELL," said he, "I've played cricket of all kinds short of county matches; but for downright fun I know nothing to beat the cricket we had on an ocean tramp in the Mediterranean one June and July. She was a steam vessel of some three thousand odd tons, out from England with coals, back from a Greek port with iron ore. I was supercargo, nominally purser, with wages of one shilling a month—I have my discharge still, a very valuable document. It was perfect weather all the way, smooth seas, and blazing hot till the evening came. Then, for a couple of hours, running about was just tolerable.

"For the first few days we were learning each other, the officers and I, and nothing much was done except talking. It was off Cape St Vincent, I think, that cricket was suggested. The second engineer began it—we were Sussex men, he and I—and the fine possibilities of that luckless county were our conversational meeting ground. One afternoon he said, 'By Jingo, I could do with a game myself now.' 'Why not?' I said, and the thing was done. Our mate bestirred himself in making a bat, the second mate cut some stumps, and fitted them in a wooden stand. Our captain sewed up a potato in canvas. After tea we began. No one stayed in long, three balls went overboard, and the bat smashed on the iron deck; but the fever held on, and the next evening saw new and better balls, and in place of the mate's broken bat, which was wider than the three stumps, and dead against M.C.C. laws, the chief engineer produced an ashen hammer-shaft, tough as steel. I superintended the ball department, and the marks are on my hands to this hour—look! those scars are the remains of half-a-dozen blisters. I got them rounding a couple of blocks of wood with a pocket-knife. Then we packed the blocks into engine waste, bound them round with twine, and squeezed them into the toes of an old pair of the second mate's socks, sewing the whole thing over with thread. They were wonderful balls, but too lively; we found it better to return to a basis of potato or dried lemon, something we couldn't lift overboard so easily.

"We played regularly after this, except when in port. We played in sight of the Rock; we played under shadow of Etna, while the silver smoke went up; we played amid the islands of the Grecian Archipelago. Every evening we played, until the red sun, dipping into the horizon, told us it was time to draw stumps, for darkness comes quickly down there. Some of us grew into stonewallers, I can tell you.

"I expect my average was the best, because I played with a straight bat, which gives a man a big pull when he's using a hammer-shaft, but the mate ran me close. Slow bowling did the trick, but it took some of them a long time to see this; at first the mate used to put those old puddings in like cannon-balls. The first few times everyone was bowled out; but as we progressed we rose to such refinement as catches in the field, then to catches at the wicket, and finally to stumping. Also we learnt to keep the ball down. In the earlier games, too, our innings were short, but it became necessary in the end to limit a man to thirty balls. How many balls we used altogether, I can't say, but we worked steadily through the old socks of the second mate (who set this sublime example of self-sacrifice), the mate, and the third engineer, and when the rolling of the Bay put an end

to the season, we had used both legs and part of the slack
of an old pair of the second engineer's trousers.

"Yes, Lord's for science, if you like, but the deck of the
Alhena for fun."

Willow and Leather.   1898

JACK

[A verse from a longer poem].

How good he was at cricket, too!
On the long evenings he would saunter to the green and
    watch the lads at play,
And by-and-by someone would offer him a few knocks.
Then the Doctor's coat would be carefully detached, and
    Jack would spit on his hands and brandish the bat,
And away the balls would go, North and South and East
    and West,
And sometimes bang into the zenith.
For Jack had little science:
Upon each ball he made the same terrific and magnificent
    onslaught,
Whether half-volley, or full-pitch, or long-lop, or leg-
    break, or off-break, or shooter, or yorker.
And when the stumps fell he would cheerfully set them up
    again, while his white teeth flashed in the recesses of
    his beard.

Willow and Leather.   1898

CRICKET ON THE ICE

EARLY in 1891, during the very hard frost that then gripped the country, cricket on the ice was played in various parts of Sussex—at Horsted Keynes, at Cuckfield, and at Sheffield Park. The Sheffield Park match is historic by reason of the inclusion of several county players.

The precise date of the Sheffield Park match was January 17th, and the two captains were Harry Phillips, the old Sussex wicket-keeper, and G. H. Lynn, a local cricketer well known in East Sussex. Phillips won the toss and decided to bat. There was a little chaff at this. "You should put them in, Phil," said one, "the wicket's so wet." "Don't bat, Phil," cried another, "it's simply a mass of water!" But the little man laughed and had his way. Two other Sussex veterans—Walter Humphreys, the lob bowler, and Jesse Hide—were chosen to open the batting, and amid cheers they slithered to the wicket. Stubberfield, an old Sussex professional of an earlier period, umpired, majestic with a birch broom, and a bunch of red flannel round his right foot. The fieldsmen were distributed pretty much as they liked. Only three or four were on skates.

"Play, play, play!" cried Stubber (as he is familiarly called) at half-past twelve, and George Bean sent down the first ball. Bean was almost as much at home on the ice as on the grass, and bowled with his usual delivery; but W. Payne, at the other end, put in cautious lobs. Jesse Hide, who had swathed his boots in sacking, had the appearance of a gouty giant. The first ball was taken by Butt at the wicket; the next shot by, and was missed by long-stop. One run was scored. There should have been a couple, only Walter Humphreys was slipping about on his heels and shouting, "No, no! I can't turn." It was a pitifully truthful statement: on the ice a booted runner cannot turn. The third ball sent Humphreys' bat to square-leg; the fourth just eluded Butt's fingers, so that the reach over-balanced him and he ingloriously fell; and the fifth was cut to the boundary for two. Then Jesse Hide had another try. Everyone has heard his stentorian "Go back!" on county grounds; on the ice he cried ten times louder. Only he did not there call "Go back!" for it is useless, but "Come on!" He made some good hits, including one for four, before he was run out. Walter Humphreys was run out too.

Charlwood and Clark took their places, and the former showed really capital style. Bean won two-thirds of a hat by bowling Clark and Bailey with successive balls. Clark had made four, and Bailey strode in intending at least to equal that score. He stood, bat in hand, on the treacherous crease, and waited for the ball. It came. There was a loud rattle, and all three stumps and the block of wood they were fixed in were seen scooting away in the direction of Tun-bridge Wells. Bailey was out. A. Payne then joined Charlwood, and they collared the bowling entirely, and gave their opponents plenty of healthy exercise. One man in particular was made busy. There was a dogged per-verseness about him that seemed to encourage the batsmen. While others of his colleagues were thankful if they could stop and return the ball on their feet, he seemed to be saddened if he kept upright. He was faithful to the notion that the best fielding is done on the back of the head. Perhaps he once saw Mr Royle field that way. Anyhow, he put his principles into practice, and must have done a mile at least on the back of his head during the game. In

o

whatever part of the lake you might be you would be sure to hear a dull thud every few minutes, followed by a peal of laughter. It was his head. Other fieldsmen were not much less unlucky. Once, a very tempting catch was sent to mid-on. He forgot all about his skates and leaped high into the air to grab the ball, with his right hand high up. He failed to reach it, and then began to come down again. He came down flat.

When Charlwood had made 30 and A. Payne 33, they retired. Osborne, who followed, did not stay very long; and then Watson and the captain were together. Now, when Harry Phillips was on his feet, he batted excellently, showing, in fact, some of the form that so electrified the Australians in 1884; but—the pity of it!—he was hardly on his feet at all. It is no exaggeration to say that of the twenty minutes he was in he spent five on his stomach, five on his back, and three on his knees. Harry was one of the few players who wore skates, and though he could skuttle as well as anyone there, he could not pirouette. Cricket on the ice demands pirouetting. Watson was only a little better. Yet, in spite of their falls and flounderings, Butt could not put down their wickets. One exciting series of overthrows ended in a tableau that everybody present must regret was not photographed. Phillips, on his hands and knees, two yards from the wickets, was tearing away at the yielding surface of the ice with his nails, trying in vain to get some purchase; he had flung his bat away long before. Butt, two yards behind the wickets, spread out as though he had been rolled, was also wriggling. Harry Phillips got in first.

When Watson's score was 9 and the captain's 5, and the total 109, exclusive of extras (which, after having run into four figures, had been disregarded by the scorers), for seven

wickets, the bell rang for luncheon; and forty sportsmen
ran up the hill to the Pavilion filled with as fine a hunger as
ever fell to the lot of man.

In winter, with the thermometer registering ten degrees
of frost, a cricket lunch is a more serious enterprise than
the summer's hasty "cold collation". Hence it was half-
past three before the teams were again in the "field", and
what little light there remained was needed for a photo-
graph. So cricket was stopped for the day, and the match
was never played out. The score of Phillips's side (irrespec-
tive of uncountable extras) read:

W. Humphreys, run out	5
J. Hide, run out	14
Charlwood, retired	30
Clark, b Bean	4
Bailey, b Bean	0
A. Payne, retired	33
Osborne, b Bean	9
H. Phillips (captain), not out . . .	5
Watson, not out	9
Total (for seven wickets) . .	109

Major Markwick and H. Christ did not bat.

The following was Lynn's side:

G. H. Lynn (captain), G. Bean, W. Payne, H. Butt,
W. Quaife, W. G. Quaife, Skinner, Kellow, J. Gilbert,
Maplesden, T. Christmas, H. Webber, and Hounsell.

The match, though cut short, had, however, progressed
sufficiently far to enable the observer to note the following
points of difference between the winter and the summer
game:

In summer, the fieldsmen pick up a ball as it rolls; in
winter, they wait till the ball stops, which may be a
matter of minutes, and then describe an arc round it,
and pick it up at the finish of the curve.

In summer, they throw it in as they run; in winter, they sit down first.

In summer, when a man is out the fieldsmen exchange catches; in winter they cut figures of eight or make an excursion down the pond.

In summer, the bowlers take a run before making their attack; in winter, they stand as still as possible, press their knees together, and thank Heaven if they can get rid of the ball without falling.

In summer, the umpires, wearing white coats, walk sedately to their places; in winter, wearing ulsters, they slide thither.

In summer, the umpires do not carry spirituous liquors in stone jars.

In summer, the cricketers leave their pipes in the Pavilion; in winter, they puff at them as they play.

In summer, the batsmen, in running, just touch the popping crease with the tip of their bats and hurry back again; in winter, they shoot a dozen yards past the bowling crease, beat the ice with their feet, wave their arms round their heads, plunge their bodies backwards and forwards, and then start for the other wicket.

In summer, a man sometimes is caught out.

It will be seen that cricket on the ice is more exciting than cricket on the turf.

Willow and Leather.   1898

THE ENGLISH GAME

How to explain the fascination that cricket exerts? It is not simple. That it should attract the proficient is understandable, although they are liable to continual mischances and mortifications such as no other game presents; but the curious thing is that it attracts the incompetents as well; those who never make a run, and cannot bowl, and yet, doomed only to dreary waiting in the pavilion and to fatiguing fielding, turn up punctually on every occasion, hoping for the best, and even (such is the human heart's buoyancy) expecting it. There is no other game at which the confirmed duffer is so persistent and so undepressed. It is for the experts, victims of misfortune, that depression waits; it is they who chew the cud of bitterness.

The phrase about "the glorious uncertainty of cricket" applies to the individual as much as to the fortunes of the struggle. For there is no second chance: the batsman who is out first ball must retire to the pavilion and brood on his ill-luck until it is time to field and forget it—when, as likely as not, he will miss a catch and enter purgatory again. The lawn-tennis player, no matter how badly he is playing, completes the set; the footballer, no matter how inept, kicks again; the polo player and the hockey player, though covered with shame, are assured of their full afternoon's sport. But it may easily be the best batsman's fate to have nothing to do but watch more fortunate batsmen receiving easier bowling than he did. This constant risk of making no runs would, you would think, deflect boys and men from the game. But no. The cricketing temperament, always slightly sardonic, accepts it. The uncertainty spells also glory.

213

There is also, still further to nourish this sardonic tendency, the weather. No game depends more upon friendly atmospheric conditions, and no game therefore is so frequently spoiled. One wonders sometimes if England may not have had a totally different climate when cricket was chosen as its national summer game; for one reads little of rain in the accounts of early matches. Were we to choose again should we again select cricket? The answer, I am sure, is yes, so undefeatable is our optimism; but surely there are more clouds than there used to be?

The conditions of the game are unique and fascinating. No other game lasts so long: Test matches are often played to a finish; first-class matches are spread over three days of changing fortunes which every ball may affect; the village match occupies four or five hours, equally packed with drama. If it is exciting to watch the ups and downs of these struggles, where the proverbial glorious uncertainty of the game is ever present, think what it must be to be one of the two-and-twenty participants. And under propitious skies how benign are the circumstances of the struggle! The sun shines, the turf is warm and scented. But perhaps, when all is said, the secret of the spell of cricket lies in the possibilities of every ball. The bat awaiting the ball is indeed an implement of destiny, but the ball which the bat awaits is more fateful. In its flight through the air, after it has left the bowler's hand and before it reaches the batsman, the spectator can live a lifetime.

The mechanics of cricket are, I imagine, now fixed. There will be no new strokes; no new varieties of bowling; all that the law-givers of the M.C.C. will have to do in the future is to deal with minor details and the politics and finance of the game: the control of Test teams, the county championship and so forth. But these are trifles. Let us do

honour to the giants, let us go to see them when we ourselves are past playing and even when we are young and
emulous; but gate-money cricket remains spectacular and
apart. Cricket is not the county ground, although that
may be the Heaven on which every boy's eyes are fixed;
cricket is the backyard, the garden, the playground, the
school field, the club and college ground, and, above all,
the village green.

"Oh," wrote an old enthusiast to me during the period
of strife at Adelaide early in this year (not of Grace) 1933—
"Oh, all this psychology! I like better the local match on a
small ground where all the better balls were hit into the
hayfield and lost. In despair a pudding was produced and
a hefty butcher smote it so violently that he knocked the
cover clean off it. The cover was caught by the wicket-
keeper, but the core was missed by point. And the deuce
and all arose. Was he out or not? I say he wasn't, putting
the case before the cover. But never mind—that's cricket,
and it's the reason why the game will always be loved in
spite of journalists and prizes to readers. There's something
about cricket that defeats snobs and conquers the press-
gang. It's a lovely game, is now and ever will be."

Should every county ground be closed and never another
shilling of gate-money leave our pockets, cricket would
still be in England's lifeblood, drawing its undismayable
devotees from every section of the nation: the cricket that
has such a hold on the young that they take their bats to
bed with them, and on the old that they cannot see half a
dozen urchins in the street, with only a lamp-post for
stumps, without pausing for a minute or two to watch; the
cricket that stirs up such a turmoil of hopes and fears in
our breasts that to consult the barometer can be almost an
anguish.

English Leaves. 1933

THE VISIONARY TRIUMPH

"THIS," he said (we were discussing our favourite dreams), "is mine." We prepared to listen.

"It is always," he went on, "the same—a cricket match: and the older I get and less able to play cricket, the oftener I have it. It is a real match, you must understand—first-class cricket, with thousands of spectators and excitement; and it is played a very long way from my home. That is an important point, as I will explain.

"I am merely one of the spectators. How long I have been watching I cannot say, but the match is nearing the end, and our side—the side which has my sympathies—is nearly all out, but still needs a few runs to win.

"What the side is I cannot clearly tell; all I know is that it is my own county, I mean the county from which I come—say Kent—and the match is at Old Trafford or Bramall Lane, against either Lancashire or Yorkshire. But the important thing is that my side is a man short. This man either has been taken ill or has had to go away because of a bereavement. I am not clear as to that, but he is not there, anyway, and unless a substitute can be found Kent will be at a disadvantage and may lose."

We all got ready to speak.

"Oh, yes," he interpolated hurriedly, "I know, of course, that a substitute may not bat for another at the end of a match, but this is a dream, remember. That, perhaps, is what dreams are for—to provide the limited and frustrated life of the daytime with the compensation of limitless adventure and success."

"Order!" we cried.

"I beg pardon," he said, and returned to the vernacular.

"Very well; that is the situation. Meanwhile the last two batsmen are in—the Kent captain and another: that is to say, the last two, unless another is forthcoming. And still there are six runs needed—five to tie and six to win. The excitement is appalling. Every one in the vast concourse is tense. It is at this moment that the captain is bowled."

He stopped to wipe his forehead.

"What happens then?" he continued. "You would think the match was over. So it would be on any ordinary ground and under ordinary conditions; but this is a dream. What happens therefore is that the Kent captain, instead of returning to the Pavilion, stops and talks to the other captain and then he leaves the pitch and begins to walk towards the ring. When he reaches the ring, some way from me, he begins to ask loudly, 'Is there a Kent man here who can play at all and would help us out?' I can hear him at first only faintly; then, as he gets closer, I can hear more clearly, 'Is there a Kent man here who can play at all and would help us out?' My heart beats faster and faster and I am nearly suffocated with suspense as he approaches, because I am a Kent man who can bat a bit, and to play for my county has always been my desire, and I am afraid that some one else will volunteer before the captain reaches me.

"You see now why the match has to be played so far away from home. If it were Kent *v.* Middlesex at Lord's, for example, there would be loads of Kentish men on the ground. But not so many up in the North.

"I always wonder why the captain does not begin in the Pavilion, but he does not. He comes straight to the ring. Every moment he is drawing nearer and no one has offered himself; and then at last he gets to me and I stand up and say that Kent is my county and I can play a bit and would like to help. He hastens to accept my offer, and I take his bat and pads and gloves and go to the pitch, amid the cheers of the crowd.

"At the wicket I am received with hearty greetings by the rival captain (this is a dream, remember), and I take middle. Then I look round the field with perfect composure, as I have always seen the best batsmen do, and have always wanted to do myself. I am the coolest thing there.

"The situation is electrical. Six runs are needed and I am the last man. The bowler against me is a demon and I am dead out of practice and by no means fond of being hit on the body. He begins his run towards the wicket, and the ball leaves his terrible long swinging arm and comes towards me like a shell. I raise my bat, get it on the half-volley right in the middle, hit it clean over the Pavilion for six, and the match is won.

"That is my favourite dream."

"No wonder," we said.

The Phantom Journal. 1919

ALLEVIATION

MORE mighty than the bat, the pen,
   And mightier still as we grow old,
And hence I needs must scribble when
   I'd fain be bowling—or be bowled.
Yet thoughts, whate'er the task, will stray,
   To work they never wholly yield;
And mine, on every sunny day,
   Are in the field, are in the field!

Willow and Leather.   1898

THE PAVILION LIBRARY

New Titles

Cricket All His Life
E. V. Lucas

The Cricket Captains of England
Alan Gibson

Backlist

Farewell to Cricket
Don Bradman

Jack Hobbs
Ronald Mason

In Celebration of Cricket
Kenneth Gregory

The Best Loved Game
Geoffrey Moorhouse

Bowler's Turn
Ian Peebles

Lord's 1787–1945
Sir Pelham Warner

Lord's 1946–1970
Diana Rait Kerr and Ian Peebles

P. G. H. Fender
Richard Streeton

Through the Caribbean
Alan Ross

Hirst and Rhodes
A. A. Thomson

Two Summers at the Tests
John Arlott

Double Century
Ed. Marcus Williams

Sort of a Cricket Person
E. W. Swanton

End of an Innings
Denis Compton

Ranji
Alan Ross

Batter's Castle
Ian Peebles

The Ashes Crown the Year
Jack Fingleton

Life Worth Living
C. B. Fry

Cricket Crisis
Jack Fingleton

Brightly Fades The Don
Jack Fingleton

Cricket Country
Edmund Blunden

Odd Men In
A. A. Thomson

Crusoe on Cricket
R. C. Robertson-Glasgow

Benny's Green's Cricket Archive